MARYLAND PHARM.

MPJE COMPREHENSIVE REVIEW

Gibson Thomas, PharmD

Second Edition

Table of Contents   **Pages**

PART ONE

PART TWO

PART-ONE

MARYLAND PHARMACY LAW

Subtitle 34. BOARD OF PHARMACY

- An institutional pharmacy shall obtain required permits in compliance with State and federal laws and regulations.

- An institutional pharmacy shall:

- Staff a pharmacist at each decentralized pharmacy site within the building or pavilion in which it is located; and

- List decentralized pharmacy sites within the building in which it is located, on the initial application, or on the renewal application.

- A decentralized pharmacy that meets the definition as set forth in this chapter may operate under the same permit as the institutional pharmacy located in the same building or pavilion.

- If full-service pharmacy services are provided to discharge patients, employees, clinic patients, or others, an institutional pharmacy shall obtain a full-service pharmacy permit.

- Any other pharmacy that does not meet the requirements of a decentralized pharmacy and is located on the campus or affiliated with an institutional pharmacy shall be separately licensed.

Sec. 10.34.03.07. Physical Requirements and Equipment

- The institutional pharmacy shall have floor space, shelving, and equipment to ensure that drugs and supplies within the institutional pharmacy are properly stored and prepared with respect to sanitation, temperature, light, ventilation, moisture control, segregation, and security.

- The institutional pharmacy shall have professional and technical equipment, supplies, and adequate physical facilities for proper compounding, dispensing, and storage of drugs.

- The institutional pharmacy shall have reference materials as required by COMAR 10.34.07.03 to enable personnel to prepare and dispense drugs properly and perform pharmaceutical care functions.

- The institutional pharmacy shall store alcohol and flammables in areas that meet basic local building code requirements for the storage of volatiles and such other laws, ordinances, or regulations as may apply.

- An institutional pharmacy that provides parenteral preparations shall comply with COMAR 10.34.19.

- The institutional pharmacy shall dispose of hazardous materials consistent with State and federal laws and regulations.

- The institutional pharmacy is responsible for the maintenance of the institution's automated medication systems in compliance with COMAR 10.34.28

Sec. 10.34.03.08. Responsibilities of Director of Pharmacy

The director of pharmacy or designee shall:

- Be responsible for the safe and efficient dispensing, control, security, and accountability of drugs.

- Work in cooperation with the other professional staff of the institutional facility with respect to the duties listed in this regulation and in ordering, administering, and controlling drug products and materials, including prescription blanks.

- Supervise the preparation of parenteral and other medications compounded within the institutional facility.

- Provide written policies and procedures to hospital professional and technical staff with regard to admixtures prepared within the institution outside of the institutional pharmacy including, but not limited to:

  o Establishing policies and procedures for preparation and handling of the admixtures; and

  o Providing incompatibility information with respect to the admixtures.

- Recommend specifications for procurement, storage and disposal of drugs, chemicals, and biologicals administered to patients to the appropriate committee of the institutional facility as determined by the governing body.

- Participate in the development of a formulary for the facility.

- Establish procedures for the development of a standard format and ongoing procedures for checking the accuracy and placement of labels on medications throughout the institution.

- Maintain and make available an inventory of antidotes and other emergency drugs, both in the pharmacy and in patient care areas, as well as:

  o Current antidote information.

- Telephone numbers of a regional poison information center.

- Other emergency assistance organizations; and

- Such other materials and information as may be considered necessary by the governing body of the institutional facility.

o   Maintain records of transactions of the institutional pharmacy as may be required by applicable law and as may be necessary to maintain accurate control and accountability for pharmaceuticals.

o   Participate in those aspects of the institutional facility's quality assurance and improvement program which relate to medication safety and pharmaceutical utilization and effectiveness.

o   Participate in teaching or research programs, or both, in the institutional facility as required.

o   Implement the policies, procedures, and decisions of the governing body of the institutional facility.

o   Ensure that a system is in place that provides a safe, secure, and efficient distribution system for pharmaceutical products within the facility.

o   Ensure that the institutional pharmacy meets inspection and other requirements of Health Occupations Article, Title 12, Annotated Code of Maryland, and these regulations.

o   Develop and implement policies and procedures to ensure that discontinued and outdated drugs and drug containers with worn, illegible, or missing labels are returned to the pharmacy for proper disposition.

o   Establish policies and procedures for identification, handling, storage, and disposition of medications brought into the institution by the patients.

o   Conduct an on-going plan for a quality assurance program that will review and evaluate pharmaceutical services and recommend improvements in these services.

- Establish policies and procedures for identification and handling of investigational drugs that include the provision of pharmacologic and toxicologic information to the medical and nursing staff according to institutional policies.

- Arrange for the inspection of drug storage areas throughout the institution on a monthly basis and maintain written records of these reviews; and

- Participate in developing and monitoring the policies and procedures pertaining to:

- Administration of drugs at an institutional facility to ensure that only authorized individuals administer drugs; and

- Self-administration of drugs not on the hospital formulary by patients to ensure that the:

  - Administration occurs in accordance with procedures established by the appropriate committee of the institution; and

  - That the self-administration is ordered by an authorized prescriber.

Sec. 10.34.03.09. Medication Packaging: Record Keeping

- A licensed pharmacist shall verify the selection of medication to be packaged and verify the completed packaging of medication performed by a registered pharmacy technician for the following:

  - Accuracy.

  - Completeness:

  - Appropriateness; and

  - Compliance with the U.S. Food and Drug Administration and current United States Pharmacopeia approved packaging.

- Packaging from the Manufacturer's Original Container. The pharmacy shall use a master log with respect to drugs that are packaged within the pharmacy facility from the original manufacturer's container which includes the:

  o Lot number assigned by the distributor or manufacturer.

  o Manufacturer's expiration date.

  o Manufacturer.

  o Lot number assigned by the pharmacy.

  o Quantity packaged.

  o Expiration date as defined in §C of this regulations.

  o Generic name of the drug.

  o Strength.

  o Date of packaging.

  o Name of person packaging; and

  o Initials of verifying licensed pharmacist.

- Unless the licensed pharmacist has reason to reduce the time period, the expiration date of the medication is the lesser of:

  o Twelve months from the date of packaging.

  o The manufacturers or distributor's listed expiration date; or

  o The maximum time period allowed for the specific packaging used for the medication.

- The licensed pharmacist shall ensure that labeling of the medication container includes the:

  o Generic name of the medication.

  o Brand name of the medication, if appropriate

  o Strength of the medication, if appropriate.

  o Lot number of the distributor or manufacturer.

- Expiration date of the medication; and

- Beyond use date of the medication, if appropriate.

Sec. 10.34.03.10. Labeling for Use Outside the Institutional Facility

- The director of pharmacy or designee shall ensure that the labels on drugs dispensed for use outside the facility by an institutional pharmacy to clinics, ambulatory patients, or other patients about to be discharged meet the requirements of Health Occupations Article, §12-505, Annotated Code of Maryland.

- The director of pharmacy or designee shall ensure that the labels contain other information that may be required by federal or State law or regulations including, but not limited to, cautionary information.

Sec. 10.34.03.11. Drug Dispensing — Emergency Supplies and Procedures

- The director of pharmacy shall participate in the development and maintenance of the formulary for emergency drugs and supplies that are maintained throughout the institutional facility.

- The director of pharmacy or designee shall, in conjunction with the medical staff of the institutional facility, develop and implement written policies and procedures to ensure compliance with the provisions of this regulation.

- The institutional pharmacy shall furnish emergency drugs and supplies only if:

  - The emergency drugs and supplies are stored in an environment which:

  - Maintains the integrity of the drugs; and

  - Provides accessibility only to authorized personnel.

- The institution follows a policy that drugs will be dispensed from the emergency drugs and supplies formulary only upon written or verbal order by an authorized prescriber.

- The emergency drugs and supplies are stocked and maintained in a manner that complies with the standards of applicable State law.

- The emergency drugs and supplies are:

  - Stored and secured:

    - With a tamper evident seal; or

    - Via electronic means; and

  - Kept in a secure area.

- The emergency drugs and supplies are labeled as follows:

  - Clearly indicating that the emergency drugs and supplies are for use in emergencies only;

  - Listing the expiration dates of the emergency drugs and supplies.

  - Listing the name or initials of the pharmacist who checked the emergency drugs and supplies; and

  - Highlighting the expiration date of the medication with the shortest expiration date.

- When the emergency drugs and supplies are contained within an emergency cart, the pharmacist checking the emergency cart shall ensure that the exterior of the cart is labeled with the:

  - Contents of the emergency cart; and

  - Name or initials of the pharmacist; and

- The director of pharmacy or designee shall ensure that repackaged drugs contained in emergency drugs and supplies are labeled:

  o In accordance with Regulation .10 of this chapter; and

  o With other information as may be required by the medical staff.

  o Upon notification that emergency drugs and supplies have been opened, a pharmacist or registered pharmacy technician shall:

- Restock the emergency drugs and supplies; or

- Provide a replacement supply.

- The director of pharmacy or designee shall ensure:

  ✓ That the expiration date of emergency drugs and supplies is the earliest date of expiration of any drug supplied; and

  ✓ Before the expiration date, the pharmacist or designee shall replace the expired drug and relabel the emergency drugs and supplies as provided in §C(5) of this regulation.

Sec. 10.34.03.12. Drug Dispensing — Prescribers' Orders

- Drugs may be dispensed from the institutional pharmacy only in response to medication orders issued by prescribers who have been authorized to do so by law and by the governing body of the institution.

- Documentation.

  o Institutional Medication Protocols.

  o The pharmacist may dispense, or make available, drugs for an approved institutional medication protocol if conditions designated by the institution are met.

- The director of pharmacy or designee shall assist in establishing institutional policies and procedures governing the development of order-sets for each individual situation for which institutional medication protocol orders exist.

- The appropriate committee of the institution shall approve any order-sets before the pharmacist may provide the medications based on the institutional medication protocol.

- A pharmacist may provide medications based on orders which do not contain unapproved abbreviations as published by the appropriate committee of the institutional facility.

- The director of pharmacy or designee shall ensure that authorized personnel have access to patient information necessary for drug monitoring including the patient's:

  - Sex.

  - Age.

  - Weight.

  - Height.

  - Diagnosis.

  - Medication and food allergies.

  - Pregnancy and lactation status.

  - Vaccination status; and

  - Name.

Sec. 10.34.03.13. Controlled Dangerous Substances

Drug Accountability.

- o The director of pharmacy is responsible for establishing procedures and maintaining adequate written or electronic records regarding dispensing and accountability of controlled dangerous substances which specify at least the following:
  - Name and strength of the drug.
  - Dose.
  - Dosage form.
  - Prescriber.
  - Patient name with second identifier.
  - Date and time of administration; and
  - Individual administering the drug.
- The director of pharmacy shall be responsible for establishing and maintaining adequate procedures for documentation of:
  - o Recording of receipt of delivery to the pharmacy.
  - o Entering into pharmacy inventory.
  - o Receiving into Schedule II inventory; and
  - o Dispensing of controlled dangerous substances, Schedule II - Schedule V.
- The director of pharmacy or designee shall be responsible for establishing and maintaining adequate procedures for documenting partially administered controlled dangerous substances:
  - o For disposal by hospital policy; and
  - o Return of unused drugs to the pharmacy.

- The director of pharmacy or designee shall establish procedures to ensure that controlled dangerous substance records include the handwritten or electronic signature of the individual authorized:
  - By the institution to dispose of drugs or to return them to the pharmacy; and
  - To witness the disposal, as defined by the institution's policies and procedures.
  - Storage and Security in the Institutional pharmacy.
- On at least a monthly basis, a pharmacist or registered pharmacy technician shall perform a physical count of each Schedule II controlled dangerous substance in the pharmacy and shall then compare that count with the perpetual inventory maintained by the pharmacy with reference to each drug.
- On at least a monthly basis, the director of pharmacy or designee shall:
  - Investigate discrepancies within the pharmacy.
  - Report losses as required by law; and
  - Take appropriate action; and
- The director of pharmacy or designee shall establish a procedure by which previously dispensed controlled dangerous substances that are no longer necessary for medical reasons are returned to the pharmacy.
- Storage and Security in the Institution. The director of pharmacy shall develop policies that only permit the dispensing of controlled dangerous substances when the following security precautions exist in the institution and the pharmacy:
  - Access to controlled dangerous substances outside the pharmacy is restricted to authorized personnel approved by institutional policy.
  - Controlled dangerous substances stored outside the pharmacy are accounted for at least at the change of each shift by licensed personnel authorized by the institution,

unless a controlled access automated dispensing system provides an on-demand report of a perpetual inventory; and

- o A pharmacist reviews the discrepancies in counts of controlled dangerous substances previously reported by other professional personnel.

Sec. 10.34.03.14. Drug Recalls Latest

- The director of pharmacy or designee shall develop and implement a drug recall procedure that can be readily activated to assure that drugs which have been recalled are returned to the pharmacy for proper disposition.

- If a recall has been initiated for a drug that has been purchased by the institution, the director of pharmacy or designee shall issue a notice in a timely manner informing affected departments of the institution that the drug shall be returned to the pharmacy for proper return or disposal.

- The institutional pharmacy is responsible for the timely retrieval of affected drugs.

Sec. 10.34.03.15. Adverse Drug Events

- The director of pharmacy or designee shall participate in the appropriate committee or committees to establish procedures to report and record adverse drug events including medication errors and adverse drug reactions.

- The director of pharmacy or designee shall immediately report adverse drug events to the prescriber, or the prescriber's designee, and make a written or electronic report to the appropriate committee or committees, as determined by the governing body of the institutional facility.

- The director of pharmacy shall participate in the deliberations of the institutional committee charged with the development of the programmatic and operational changes that result from the analysis of medication errors or other adverse events.

- The director of pharmacy, in collaboration with the medical staff and other appropriate departments and services, shall develop and maintain a process for training staff regarding detecting and reporting medication errors to prevent future occurrences.

- The director of pharmacy or designee shall make further reports of adverse reactions as required by federal or State law.

Sec. 10.34.03.16. Pharmaceutical Care Functions of the Pharmacist

The pharmacist shall be available as necessary to provide pharmaceutical care to individual patients including, but not limited to:

- Participating in decisions about medication use for patients including decisions not to use medication therapy as well as judgments about:
  o Medication selection.
  o Dosages.
  o Routes and methods of administration.
  o Medication therapy monitoring; and
  o The provision of medication-related information and counseling to individual patients.

- Cooperating directly with health care professionals and the patient in designing, implementing, and monitoring a therapeutic outcome.

- Providing care directly to the patient to improve a patient's quality of life through achieving definite and predefined, medication-related therapeutic outcomes such as:

- o Curing the disease.

- o Eliminating or reducing a symptomatology.

- o Arresting or slowing a disease process.

- o Preventing a disease or symptomatology; and

- o Improving patient's quality of life.

- Identifying potential and actual medication-related problems, resolving actual medication-related problems, and preventing potential medication-related problems caused by:

  - o Untreated indications.

  - o Improper drug selection.

  - o Sub-therapeutic dosage.

  - o Failure to received medication.

  - o Over dosage.

  - o Adverse drug reactions.

  - o Drug interactions, including drug-drug, drug-food, drug-laboratory test interactions; and

  - o Medication uses without appropriate indication.

Sec. 10.34.03.17. Requirements for a Decentralized Pharmacy

- A decentralized pharmacy is subject to:

  - o Health Occupations Article, Title 12, Annotated Code of Maryland.

  - o This subtitle; and

  - o Other applicable State and federal laws and regulations.

- A decentralized pharmacy shall ensure that a licensed pharmacist is immediately available on the premises of the decentralized pharmacy to:
  - Supervise pharmacy operations; and
  - Provide the final check for preparing medication orders for administration in the institutional facility.
- Notwithstanding §B of this regulation, a pharmacist assigned to a decentralized pharmacy may leave the decentralized pharmacy for a short period of time to perform pharmaceutical care functions in the institutional facility.
- A director of pharmacy of the institutional pharmacy shall be responsible for pharmacy operations involving a decentralized pharmacy, including direct supervision of decentralized pharmacy personnel by a pharmacist and compliance with this chapter.
- A pharmacy department may store prescription medications and over the counter medications that are approved for use by the institutional pharmacy as required for the treatment of patients in the nursing unit served by the decentralized pharmacy.
- An institutional pharmacy and the decentralized pharmacy shall have shared common electronic files or appropriate technology to allow access to sufficient information necessary or required to process functions required for the care of patients within the service area of the decentralized pharmacy.
- A decentralized pharmacy shall have a pharmacist physically located at the decentralized pharmacy to directly supervise pharmacy technicians and pharmacy technician trainees during hours of operation.
- An institutional pharmacy shall notify the Board in writing within 14 days of a change of location, discontinuance of service, or closure of a decentralized pharmacy.

19

- Security.

  - In addition to the security requirements outlined in COMAR 10.34.05, a decentralized pharmacy shall have adequate security and procedures to:

    - Prohibit unauthorized access.

    - Comply with federal and State regulations; and

    - Maintain patient confidentiality.

  - Access to the decentralized pharmacy shall be limited to pharmacists, pharmacy technicians, and pharmacy technician trainees employed by the institutional pharmacy, and other personnel authorized by the director of pharmacy.

Sec. 10.34.04.03. Permanent Transfer of a Prescription Between Pharmacies

A pharmacist from a primary pharmacy may permanently transfer a prescription order to a secondary pharmacy to be dispensed to a specific patient if:

- The prescription is lawfully refillable.

- The prescription is not for a Schedule II controlled dangerous substance noted in Criminal Law Article, Title 5, Subtitle 4, Annotated Code of Maryland.

- The pharmacist transferring the prescription from the primary pharmacy indicates on the prescription, within the prescription computer database and within any appropriate other records used for dispensing:

  - That the prescription has been permanently transferred.

  - The name of the secondary pharmacy.

  - The name of the pharmacist who transferred the prescription to the secondary pharmacy.

- o The name of the pharmacist at the secondary pharmacy to whom the prescription was transferred if the transfer occurred in an oral manner; and

- o The date on which the prescription was transferred to the secondary pharmacy.

Sec. 10.34.04.06. Outsourcing of a Prescription Order Latest version.

A pharmacist from a primary pharmacy may transmit a prescription order to a secondary pharmacy for preparation and final dispensing to a specific patient or for return to the primary pharmacy for final dispensing to a specific patient if:

- The label contains the name, address, and phone number of the primary pharmacy.

- The patient is informed in writing of the name and address of the secondary pharmacy.

- The patient is informed in writing that the prescription order was prepared at a secondary pharmacy.

- The original prescription order is filed as a prescription order at the primary pharmacy.

- The pharmacist from the primary pharmacy documents in a readily retrievable and identifiable manner:
  - o That the prescription order was prepared by a secondary pharmacy
  - o The name of the secondary pharmacy.
  - o The name of the pharmacist who transmitted the prescription order to the secondary pharmacy.
  - o The name of the pharmacist at the secondary pharmacy to whom the prescription order was transmitted if the transmission occurred in an oral manner.
  - o The date on which the prescription was transmitted to the secondary pharmacy; and
  - o The date on which the medication was sent to the primary pharmacy.

- o Both the primary and secondary pharmacies are licensed in this State, or operated by the federal government; and

- o The primary pharmacy maintains, in a readily retrievable and identifiable manner, a record of preparations received from the secondary pharmacy.

Sec. 10.34.04.07.

Documentation by the Secondary Pharmacy when a Prescription Order is Outsourced

The permit holder at the secondary pharmacy is responsible for maintaining documentation in a readily retrievable and identifiable manner, which includes:

- That the prescription order was transmitted from another pharmacy.

- The name and information identifying the specific location of the primary pharmacy.

- The name of the pharmacist who transmitted the prescription to the secondary pharmacy if the transmission occurred in an oral manner.

- The name of the pharmacist at the secondary pharmacy who accepted the transmitted prescription order.

- The name of the pharmacist at the secondary pharmacy who prepared the prescription order.

- The date on which the prescription order was received at the secondary pharmacy; and

- The date on which the prepared product was sent to the primary pharmacy if it was sent back to the primary pharmacy.

Sec. 10.34.04.08.

Preparation of Stock and Investigational Medications

- A pharmacist may provide medication for use as stock medication for a licensed health care facility in accordance with applicable laws, if the pharmacy providing the medication also serves as the primary provider of patient specific medication for the facility.

- A pharmacist may provide medication for use as stock medication for final dispensing or administration by an authorized prescriber who is permitted by law to administer or dispense medication if the pharmacist receives a written stock medication order from the authorized prescriber for each delivery of medication to the authorized prescriber.

- A pharmacist may prepare, package, and label investigational drugs not destined for a specific individual at the time of preparation, packaging, and labeling if:
  - The study for which medications are prepared, packaged, and labeled is approved by an institutional review board as defined in federal law; and
  - The pharmacy permit holder ensures that records disclosing the identity of the subject who eventually receives the medication are:

- Received by a pharmacist on duty at the pharmacy within 30 days after being provided to a patient: and

- Maintained in the pharmacy.

Sec. 10.34.04.09. Permit and Quality Assurance

- The permit holder of a pharmacy which prepares patient specific prescriptions as a secondary pharmacy such that these prescriptions account for 5 percent or more of the pharmacy's total number of prescriptions filled shall submit to the Board of Pharmacy, for approval by the Board or a designee of the Board, a plan detailing the steps it has taken to ensure the safety and quality of prescriptions filled as a secondary pharmacy.

- The plan under §A of this regulation shall include:
    - Measures to be taken to comply with State and federal laws.
    - The method by which each pharmacist responsible for each prescription is identified in the records.
    - Measures taken to maintain the security, integrity, and confidentiality of patient records; and
    - The establishment and maintenance of a quality assurance program.
- Except as provided in Regulation .06 of this chapter, a permit holder of a pharmacy shall obtain manufacturing and distribution permits in order to compound or package medication that is not prepared as a prescription destined for a specific patient, but is forwarded to another pharmacy, authorized prescriber, licensed distributor, or other person or entity.

Sec. 10.34.05.02. Prescription Area Latest version.

The pharmacy permit holder shall:

- Ensure that the prescription area:
- Maintains temperature and ventilation at levels that do not affect the prescription drugs or devices stored in the area; and
- Permits reasonable communication between the pharmacist and the public when the pharmacy is open.

- Provide a means of securing the prescription area

- Prevent an individual from being in the prescription area unless a pharmacist is immediately available on the premises to provide pharmacy services.

- Monitor unauthorized or emergency entry after the prescription area has been secured by the pharmacist; and

- Prevent unauthorized entry when the prescription area is closed during a period that the rest of the establishment is open.

    o The pharmacist shall:

    o Secure the prescription area and its contents in order that the pharmacy permit holder or the pharmacy permit holder's agent may:

- Monitor unauthorized or emergency entry after the prescription area has been secured by the pharmacist; and

- Prevent unauthorized entry when the prescription area is closed during a period that the rest of the establishment is open.

- Have sole possession of a means of access to the pharmacy, except in emergencies; and

- Establish a means of access for use in an emergency when the pharmacist is not available to access the prescription area.

    o Security.

- A pharmacy shall be secure from unauthorized entry as follows:

    o Access from outside the premises shall be:

        ▪ Kept to a minimum; and

        ▪ Well controlled.

- o The outside perimeter of the premises shall be well lit; and

  - o Entry into areas where prescription drugs or devices and patient records are stored shall be limited to authorized personnel.

- A pharmacy shall be equipped with:

  - o An alarm system to detect entry after hours.

  - o A security system that provides protection against theft and diversion.

  - o Appropriate software to facilitate the identification of evidence of tampering with computers or electronic records.

  - o An inventory management and control system that protects against, detects, and documents any instances of theft, diversion, or counterfeiting.

  - o A security system to protect the integrity and confidentiality of data and documents limited to authorized personnel; and

  - o A means to make the data and documentation required under this section readily available to the Board, an agent of the Board, the Division of Drug Control, or federal and other State law enforcement officials.

Sec. 10.34.05.03. Pharmacy Operation

- A pharmacist shall be immediately available on the premises to always provide pharmacy services the pharmacy is in operation.

- If the prescription area is not open the same hours as the establishment, the pharmacy permit holder shall prominently display signs indicating the business hours of the prescription area.

Sec. 10.34.05.04. Records

A pharmacy permit holder shall:

- o   Prevent unauthorized disclosure or loss by securing all patient records.

- o   Designate personnel with authorized access to computerized patient records; and

- o   Maintain current computerized records in a manner which permits reconstruction within 48 hours, except:

    - ▪   In an emergency as defined in Regulation .01 of this chapter, or

    - ▪   With the prior approval of the Board.

A pharmacy permit holder may store patient records away from the prescription area in a manner that prevents unauthorized disclosure or loss.

Sec. 10.34.06.03. Mailing Address

- •   Each licensed pharmacist, pharmacy intern, and registered pharmacy technician shall report to the Board the pharmacist's, pharmacy interns, or pharmacy technician's current mailing address on the pharmacist's, pharmacy intern's, or pharmacy technician's biennial license or registration renewal form.

- •   The mailing address:

    - o   May be the pharmacist's residence address.

    - o   Shall be the pharmacy intern's residence address; or

    - o   Shall be the pharmacy technician's residence address.

- •   Within 30 days of the date a pharmacist, pharmacy intern, or pharmacy technician changes the pharmacist's, pharmacy interns, or pharmacy technician's mailing address, the pharmacist, pharmacy intern, or pharmacy technician shall notify the Board in writing of any change in the information in §A of this regulation

Sec. 10.34.06.04. Place of Employment

- This regulation applies only to pharmacists, pharmacy interns, and pharmacy technicians employed in Maryland.

- Each licensed pharmacist, registered pharmacy intern, and registered pharmacy technician shall report to the Board the pharmacist's, pharmacy intern's, or pharmacy technician's place of employment on the pharmacist, pharmacy intern, or pharmacy technician biennial license or registration renewal form. A pharmacist, pharmacy intern, or pharmacy technician employed at more than one location shall report the primary employment location at the time the renewal form is submitted to the Board.

- Within 30 days of a change in the pharmacist's, pharmacy intern's, or pharmacy technician's primary employment location, the pharmacist, pharmacy intern, or pharmacy technician shall notify the Board in writing of any change in the information required by this regulation. If the pharmacist's, pharmacy intern's, or pharmacy technician's primary employment location changes and the pharmacist's, pharmacy intern's, or pharmacy technician's new primary employment location is owned by the same corporation, partnership, or individual owner, the pharmacist, pharmacy intern, or pharmacy technician is not required to report the change except when completing a biennial license or registration renewal form.

Sec. 10.34.07.01-1. Equipment

A pharmacy shall have the following equipment to carry out the practice of pharmacy in Maryland:

- If applicable, a Class A prescription balance and weights, or a prescription balance with equivalent or superior sensitivity to a Class A prescription balance.

- A refrigerator, solely for the storage of drugs requiring refrigeration, with a thermometer or a temperature monitoring device; and

- A freezer, if applicable.

Sec. 10.34.07.02. Additional Equipment

- The pharmacy shall maintain additional equipment to enable it to prepare and dispense prescriptions properly consistent with its scope of practice.

Sec. 10.34.07.03. Reference Libraries

- A pharmacy permit holder shall maintain an adequate reference library to enable it to prepare and dispense prescriptions properly, consistent with its scope of practice.

- A pharmacy permit holder shall maintain a library of reference sources appropriate to the type of pharmacy practice at that particular location. A pharmacy permit holder shall include in the pharmacy's library current material regarding the technical, clinical, and professional aspects of practice with emphasis in the area in which the pharmacy specializes.

- A pharmacy permit holder may utilize websites and electronic references created by established medical publishers which are recognized as standard for a particular type of pharmacy practice as a supplement to its printed library.

- A pharmacy permit holder shall maintain a library containing reference sources that:

    o Enable the pharmacist to compound medications in a safe and effective manner.

    o List the possible drug interactions and possible adverse effects of medications dispensed by the pharmacy.

    o List the therapeutic usage and dosages of medications dispensed by the pharmacy.

    o List the therapeutic equivalents for medications; and

    o Provide guidelines for the counseling of patients.

- A pharmacy permit holder that specializes in nuclear or parenteral prescriptions may limit the library it maintains pursuant to §B of this regulation to the pharmacy permit holder's area of specialization.

- A pharmacy permit holder shall maintain material safety data sheets, if applicable.

Sec. 10.34.10.01. Patient Safety and Welfare

A pharmacist shall:

- Abide by all federal and State laws relating to the practice of pharmacy and the dispensing, distribution, storage, and labeling of drugs and devices, including but not limited to:

- Verify the accuracy of the prescription before dispensing the drug or device if the pharmacist has reason to believe that the prescription contains an error; and

- Maintain proper sanitation, hygiene, biohazard precautions, and infection control when performing tasks in the prescription process.

- A pharmacist may not:

    o Engage in conduct which departs from the standard of care ordinarily exercised by a pharmacist.

- o Practice pharmacy under circumstances or conditions which prevent the proper exercise of professional judgment; or

- o Engage in unprofessional conduct.

Therapeutic Interchange.

- A pharmacist may not perform a therapeutic interchange without the prior approval of the authorized prescriber except as provided in §C(2) of this regulation.

- A pharmacist who provides a pharmacy service to a patient of a hospital, as defined in Health-General Article, §19-301, Annotated Code of Maryland, or a resident of a comprehensive care or extended care facility, as defined in COMAR 10.07.02.01B, may perform a therapeutic interchange without the prior approval of the authorized prescriber if the governing body of the hospital, comprehensive care facility, or extended care facility has established procedures for therapeutic interchange.

- This section does not permit any act not otherwise authorized by Health Occupations Article, Title 12, Annotated Code of Maryland.

Sec. 10.34.10.02. Compensation

- A pharmacy technician, pharmacy intern, or a pharmacist may not fraudulently seek or accept compensation for a pharmacy product or service not provided.

Sec. 10.34.10.03. Patient Privacy

- The pharmacy technician, pharmacy intern, pharmacist, and pharmacy permit holder shall ensure confidentiality in creating, storing, accessing, transferring, and disposing of a patient record.

- A pharmacy technician, pharmacy intern, or pharmacist may not disclose identifiable information contained in a patient's medical record:
  - Without the patient's consent.
  - Without order or direction of a court; or
  - Unless the disclosure is authorized pursuant to Health-General Article, §§4-301-4-307, Annotated Code of Maryland.

Sec. 10.34.10.04. Competence

A pharmacy technician, pharmacy intern, or a pharmacist shall:

- Maintain knowledge of the current pharmacy and drug laws and health and sanitation laws relevant to the practice of pharmacy; and
- Provide a pharmaceutical service only within the scope of the pharmacy technician's, pharmacy intern's, or pharmacist's training and education.

Sec. 10.34.10.05. Duty to Report Latest version.

- Except when the conduct in question includes drug or alcohol abuse or dependency, a pharmacy technician, pharmacy intern, or pharmacist shall report to the Board:
  - Conduct which violates a statute or regulation pertaining to the practice of pharmacy.
  - Conduct by a pharmacy technician, pharmacy intern, or pharmacist that deceives, defrauds, or harms the public; and
  - The unauthorized practice of pharmacy.
- A pharmacy technician, pharmacy intern, or pharmacist shall report to the pharmacist rehabilitation committee, as defined in Health Occupations Article, §12-317, Annotated Code

of Maryland, conduct by a pharmacist technician, pharmacy intern, or pharmacist that involves drug or alcohol abuse or dependency.

Sec. 10.34.10.06. Discrimination, Harassment, and Sexual Misconduct

- In the practice of pharmacy, a pharmacy technician, pharmacy intern, or pharmacist may not:

- Discriminate based on age, gender, race, ethnicity, national origin, religion, sexual orientation, disability, socioeconomic status, or other basis as proscribed by law; or

- Sexually harass a patient, coworker, employee, or supervisee, which includes but is not limited to an unwanted, deliberate, or repeated comment, gesture, or physical contact of a sexual nature.

Sexual Misconduct.

- A pharmacy technician, pharmacy intern, or pharmacist may not:

- Dispense or offer to dispense a prescription drug or device in exchange for:

- A sexual act such as anal intercourse, analingus, cunnilingus, fellatio, or vaginal intercourse as specified in Criminal Law Article, §3-301(e) and (g), Annotated Code of Maryland, or

- Sexual contact such as the intentional touching of an intimate part of an individual's body, whether clothed or unclothed, for the purpose of sexual arousal, gratification, abuse of either party, or penetration as specified in Criminal Law Article, §3-301(f), Annotated Code of Maryland; or

- Engage in sexual behavior including but not limited to a sexual act or sexual contact as specified in §B(1)(a) of this regulation, with a client or patient.

- In the context of a professional evaluation, treatment, procedure, or other service to the client or patient, regardless of the setting in which the professional service is provided, or

- Under the pretense of diagnostic or therapeutic intent or benefit.

- Sexual contact does not include an act commonly expressive of familial or friendly affection.

Sec. 10.34.10.07. Disposition and Return of a Prescription Drug or Device

- A pharmacist may accept the return of a properly labeled and properly sealed manufacturer's package or individual unit dose of a drug or device that the pharmacist determines to have been handled in a manner which preserves the strength, quality, purity, and identity of the drug or device during an interim period between the sale of the drug or device and its return to the pharmacy.

A pharmacist may not:

- Return to the pharmacy's stock or offer for sale a prescribed drug or device that has been previously sold and has left the pharmacy's possession except as provided in §A of this regulation; or

- Sell, give away, or otherwise dispose of a drug, drug accessory, chemical, or device if the pharmacist knows or should know that the drug, drug accessory, chemical, or device is to be used in an illegal activity.

- A pharmacy technician or pharmacy intern may not accept the return of prescription drugs or devices from a patient.

Sec. 10.34.10.08. Refusing to Dispense a Controlled Substance

- If, based on generally accepted professional standards for the practice of pharmacy, a pharmacist has reason to believe, or should have reason to believe, that a prescription for a controlled dangerous substance was not issued for a legitimate medical purpose in the usual course of the prescriber's practice, the pharmacist may not dispense the controlled dangerous substance until the pharmacist:
  - Consults with the prescriber; and
  - Verifies the medical legitimacy of the prescription.
- If, after consulting with the prescriber, and based on generally accepted professional standards for the practice of pharmacy, a pharmacist has reason to believe that the prescription for a controlled dangerous substance was not issued for a legitimate medical purpose in the usual course of the prescriber's practice, the pharmacist shall:
  - Refuse to dispense the drug; and
  - Report the incident to the regulatory board that licenses the prescriber.

Sec. 10.34.10.09. Sanctions

- The Board may take action to reprimand a licensee, place the licensee on probation, or suspend or revoke the licensee's license if the licensee commits a violation of this chapter.
- The Board may take action to reprimand a registrant, place the registrant on probation, or suspend or revoke the registrant's registration if the registrant commits a violation of this chapter.

Sec. 10.34.10.10. Whole or Substantial Ownership of a Pharmacy by an Authorized Prescriber

- In this regulation," owned wholly or substantially" means ownership of 10 percent or more of a pharmacy.

- A pharmacist may not associate as a partner, coowner, or employee of a pharmacy that is owned wholly or substantially by an authorized prescriber or group of authorized prescribers.

Chapter 10.34.12. Removal of Expired Medications

Sec. 10.34.12.01. Manufacturer's Expiration Date

- A wholesale distributor, pharmacist, or pharmacy shall distribute or hold for sale medications bearing a manufacturer's expiration date pursuant to 21 C.F.R. §211.137.

- A wholesale distributor, pharmacist, or pharmacy shall have adequate and credible provisions for return of outdated drugs, including but not limited to partials, through its wholesaler distributor or reverse distributor.

Sec. 10.34.14.02. Opening a Pharmacy

To apply for a pharmacy permit, an applicant shall:

- Submit an application to the Board on the form that the Board requires.

- Pay to the Board an application fee set by the Board in COMAR 10.34.09; and

- Submit to an opening inspection, at which time the applicant shall have, at a minimum, the following:

    - If applicable, a Class A prescription balance and weights, or a prescription balance with equivalent or superior sensitivity.

- A refrigerator, solely for the storage of medications requiring refrigeration, with a thermometer or a temperature monitoring device.

- Additional equipment to enable the pharmacy to prepare and dispense prescriptions properly consistent with the pharmacy's scope of practice.

- Hot and cold running water.

- A library of current reference sources, consistent with the pharmacy's scope of practice, that is accessible to appropriate personnel.

- A current edition of Maryland Pharmacy Laws.

- A security system in accordance with COMAR 10.34.05.02; and

- A pharmacist on the premises during the opening inspection, if prescription drugs are present.

- A pharmacy may not be located in a residence.

- A permit holder who has been issued a pharmacy permit by the Board shall, within 60 days following the initial issuance of the pharmacy permit, have and maintain an operational pharmacy.

- The Board shall inspect a pharmacy after the initial issuance of a pharmacy permit to ensure that the pharmacy is an operational pharmacy.

- If a pharmacy is not an operational pharmacy within 60 days following the initial issuance of a pharmacy permit, the Board shall notify the permit holder of the Board's intent to rescind the pharmacy permit.

- A permit holder who has been notified of the Board's intent to rescind the pharmacy permit under this regulation shall return the permit to the Board within 10 days of notification, unless the permit holder submits documentation satisfactory to the Board to show that the pharmacy is an operational pharmacy.

- If a pharmacy permit has been rescinded under this regulation, the permit holder may reapply if application requirements are met.

- The Board may waive any of the requirements set forth in this regulation.

Sec. 10.34.14.03. Information to be Included in Notification of Closing

At least 14 days before a location's anticipated date of ceasing to operate as a licensed pharmacy, the pharmacy permit holder shall: Notify the:

- Board in writing by certified mail, return receipt requested, or hand delivered to the Board's office of the day on which the licensed pharmacy will cease to operate as a pharmacy; and

- Division of Drug Control by certified mail, return receipt requested, of the day on which the licensed pharmacy will cease to operate as a pharmacy; and

- Request a closing inspection date.

- Upon notification by a pharmacy permit holder of the proposed date on which a licensed pharmacy will cease to operate, the Board shall notify the Board's agent to schedule the closing inspection in conjunction with the Board's agent, if necessary.

- The Board, or the Board's agent, shall perform the closing inspection within 72 hours of the pharmacy ceasing to operate.

Sec. 10.34.14.04. Required Information and Procedure

- At the closing inspection of a licensed pharmacy, the pharmacy permit holder shall provide to the Board, or the Board's agent, information and documentation required by Regulation .05 of this chapter.

- The pharmacy permit holder shall remove or completely cover indications that the premises was a pharmacy within 30 days after the date the licensed pharmacy ceases to operate as a pharmacy.

- The pharmacy permit holder shall notify prescription drug suppliers to the pharmacy, before ceasing to operate as a pharmacy, of the date that the location will cease to operate as a pharmacy.

- The pharmacy permit holder shall notify the public of the date that the pharmacy will cease to operate as a pharmacy by that date.

- The pharmacy permit holder shall notify the public of the location to which the patients' records have been transferred, by the date the pharmacy ceases to operate.

- If patient records are not transferred, the pharmacy permit holder shall notify the public of the:
  o Location of the patient records.
  o Method by which the patient records shall be maintained; andProcedure by which patients and other authorized individuals or entities may access the patient records.
  o The pharmacy permit holder shall comply with all federal and State laws and regulations.
  o If the Board's agent performs the closing inspection, the Board's agent shall obtain information and documentation required by Regulation .05 of this chapter.

Sec. 10.34.14.05. Information and Documentation Due at the Closing Inspection

Information and documentation due at the closing inspection shall include:

- The exact date on which the pharmacy ceased to operate as a pharmacy.

- A copy of the inventory required by the Drug Enforcement Administration.

- The pharmacy permit and Maryland Department of Health controlled dangerous substance registration for cancellation.

- The names, address, telephone numbers, and Drug Enforcement Administration registration numbers of the persons or business entities to whom any prescription drugs in stock were returned or transferred under Regulation .05 of this chapter and for any prescription files or patient records transferred.

- If prescription drugs are destroyed pursuant to Regulation .06 of this chapter, and Regulation .07 of this chapter does not apply to the prescription drugs, the pharmacy permit holder shall provide the Board with a letter, signed under oath by the pharmacy permit holder, stating the:
  - Date, place and manner in which the prescription drugs were destroyed.
  - Names, addresses, and telephone numbers of the persons responsible for destroying the prescription drugs; and
  - Name, dosage unit, and quantity of each type of prescription drug destroyed.

- If any patient records which are not required to be maintained by law, or other documents containing patient information are destroyed, the pharmacy permit holder shall provide the Board with a letter, signed under oath by the pharmacy permit holder, stating:
  - That the documents were destroyed.
  - The date of the destruction of the documents.
  - The name and address of the person who destroyed the documents.
  - That the records or other documents were destroyed in a manner so as to avoid breaches of patients' confidentiality; and
  - The identity of the records destroyed; and

- If any patient records or other documents containing patient information are transferred, the pharmacy permit holder shall provide the Board with a letter, signed under oath by the pharmacy permit holder, stating:
  - The date, time, place to which and manner in which the records or other documents were transferred.
  - The names, addresses, and telephone numbers of the persons responsible for transferring the records or other documents.
  - That the records or other documents were transferred in a manner so as to avoid breaches of patients' confidentiality; and
  - The identity of the records transferred.

Sec. 10.34.14.06. Disposition of Prescription Drugs Other than Controlled Dangerous Substances

With the exception of controlled dangerous substances, prescription drugs in stock shall be disposed of by one or more of the following means:

- Returning them to a distributor or manufacturer; or
- Transferring them to another licensed pharmacy, authorized prescriber, or other person or entity approved by the Board or the Division of Drug Control.

Subtitle 34. BOARD OF PHARMACY

Sec. 10.34.15.01. Requirements

An individual applying for licensure as a pharmacist by reciprocity shall:

- Submit to the Board an application on a form provided by the Board.

- Pay to the Board the fee as specified in COMAR 10.34.09.

- Submit to the Board evidence of completion of at least 520 hours of pharmacy experience after graduation from a school or college of pharmacy approved by the Board or accredited by the American Council on Pharmaceutical Education.

- Pass the MPJE; and

- Pass the exam of oral English competency described in COMAR 10.34.02.

- The Board shall waive the requirements of §A(5) of this regulation if the candidate for licensure by reciprocity submits to the Board written documentation that the candidate has passed an equivalent oral English competency exam in another state that was required by the other state's licensing proceduresbChapter 10.34.16. Portable Drug Kits for Licensed Home Health Agencies, Hospices, and Home Infusion Providers Licensed as Residential Services Agencies

Sec. 10.34.16.02. Requirements for Prescription Protocol

Before distributing a portable drug kit, the pharmacist shall ensure that the prescription protocol includes:

- The name, strength, and quantity of a drug to be included in the portable drug kit.

- The name of the receiving agency or designated agent.

- The directions for use.

- Conditions for use.

- Contraindications for use; and

- The signature, printed name, and telephone number of the physician authorizing the kit.

Subtitle 34. BOARD OF PHARMACY

Chapter 10.34.16. Portable Drug Kits for Licensed Home Health Agencies, Hospices, and Home Infusion Providers Licensed as Residential Services Agencies

Sec. 10.34.16.03. Records

A pharmacist shall:

- File the prescription protocol in a readily retrievable manner.

- Document the:

  o Date of distribution of the portable drug kit,

  o Name of the person or agency to whom the kit is delivered, and

  o Date of delivery for each kit distributed.

- File an administration record for all drugs administered from a kit upon return of the kit to the pharmacy; and

- Notify the Board of Pharmacy before distributing portable drug kits under this chapter.

Sec. 10.34.16.04. Requirements of the Portable Drug Kit

- The pharmacist shall ensure that the portable drug kit:

  o Is sealed with a tamper evident tag or other means for detecting entry to the kit.

  o Displays on the outside of the kit:

    ▪ A serial number unique to the kit.

- An expiration date which reflects the earliest expiration date of any item contained in the kit.

- The contents of the kit.

- That the contents are or are not sterile.

- The legend "To be returned to the pharmacy within 5 days of breaking seal, with a completed administration record or prescription enclosed": and

- Storage requirements for the contents.

- Contains:

- Only prescription drugs and nonprescription items approved for the kit by a committee as defined in Regulation .01B (1) of this chapter.

- A temperature monitor to indicate maintenance of proper storage conditions; and

- A written administration record to be completed by the licensed health care provider using the kit, which includes the administration record indicating:

  - The name of the patient,

  - The name of the prescriber,

  - Drug name, form, and dosage,

  - Date the drug was used or wasted,

  - The reason for administration or wastage of the drug, and

  - The name of the licensed health care provider utilizing the kit.

- Displays or includes written information inside the kit listing contraindications to use of the kit; and

- Does not contain a controlled dangerous substance.

o A pharmacist shall only distribute a portable drug kit which complies with the requirements of this chapter.

Subtitle 34. BOARD OF PHARMACY

Sec. 10.34.17.02. Pharmaceutical Specialty

- The Board may recognize as a pharmaceutical specialty not listed under Regulation .01B(4) of this chapter, upon written application and supporting documentation to the Board by an applicant for a waiver permit.

- When evaluating an application for a waiver pharmacy, the Board shall consider whether:

  o The pharmaceutical specialty service is necessary to meet a specific therapeutic need.

  o The location is accessible without endangering public health and safety.

  o The pharmacy is properly equipped to perform the pharmaceutical specialty.

  o The applicant has provided a full and detailed description of the pharmaceutical specialty that clearly substantiates the basis for the request of a waiver permit; and

  o A policy and procedure manual are included with the application which sets forth a detailed description of the pharmacy operation.

- No one criterion or combination of criteria listed in §B of this regulation shall be binding upon the Board.

- The Board's determination of whether a limited practice or setting constitutes a pharmaceutical specialty is final.

Subtitle 34. BOARD OF PHARMACY

Sec. 10.34.17.03. Requirements of a Waiver Pharmacy

- The Board shall issue a waiver permit to an applicant that:

    o Meets the requirements of this chapter; and

- Performs pharmaceutical specialty services:

    o Listed in Regulation .01B (4) of this chapter; or

    o Approved by the Board.

- The applicant shall:

    o Submit an application form approved by the Board.

    o Pay a fee as set forth in COMAR 10.34.09.

    o Submit any other documentation as required by the Board.

    o Employ at least one pharmacist at the applicant's proposed facility who has received education or training in the pharmaceutical specialty in addition to that required for licensure: and

    o Notify the Board in writing within 30 days of any change in the information given on the initial or renewal waiver pharmacy application.

Subtitle 34. BOARD OF PHARMACY

Sec. 10.34.17.04. Restricted Practice

- A waiver pharmacy is restricted to the pharmaceutical specialty services approved by the Board in the waiver permit.

- A waiver pharmacy may not perform functions of a full-service pharmacy.

- A full-service pharmacy may perform pharmaceutical specialty services as long as the full-service pharmacy is able to demonstrate competency in performing the pharmaceutical specialty.

- A full-service pharmacy and a waiver pharmacy may operate on the same premises provided that the full-service pharmacy and the waiver pharmacy:

  o Obtain separate permits from the Board.

  o Are supervised by separate licensed pharmacists who are responsible for the operations of their respective pharmacies at all times the pharmacies are in operation; and

- Maintain separate inventory and record keeping for each pharmacy permit.

Subtitle 34. BOARD OF PHARMACY

Chapter 10.34.18. Continuing Education for Pharmacists

- This chapter does not apply to pharmacists applying for renewal for the first renewal period following the issuance of the original license, if the pharmacist obtains a license within 1 year of the completion of the pharmacist's pharmaceutical education.

- The Board may grant an exception from the continuing education requirements if the pharmacist presents evidence that failure to comply was due to circumstances beyond the pharmacist's control.

Sec. 10.34.18.03. Requirements for Pharmacists Practicing in Maryland

- A pharmacist license expires on the last day of the pharmacist's birth month every other year

- Before the expiration date of the pharmacist's license, the pharmacist shall:

    o   File a renewal application.

    o   Pay any applicable fees; and

    o   Earn continuing pharmaceutical education (CE) credits required by this chapter.

- CE Requirements.

    o   A pharmacist licensed to practice in Maryland applying for renewal shall:

    o   Earn 30 hours of approved CE within the 2-year period immediately preceding the license expiration date that include:

        ▪   1 hour on the topic of preventing medication errors, such as appropriate dispensing of opioids; and

        ▪   2 hours of CE obtained through live instruction.

    o   Attest to the fact that the pharmacist has completed the CE requirement on a Board approved form; and

    o   Retain supporting documents for inspection by the Board for 4 years after the date of renewal for which the CE credits were used.

- A pharmacist certified to administer vaccinations in Maryland applying for renewal shall:

    o   As part of the 30 hours of approved CE requirement, complete 4 hours of CE credits related to vaccinations; or

Sec. 10.34.18.04. Requirements for Pharmacists Not Practicing in Maryland

- A licensed pharmacist not practicing in Maryland shall fulfill the continuing education requirements of Maryland.

Sec. 10.34.18.05. Requirements for Pharmacists who are Authorized Prescribers

- A pharmacist who is also an authorized prescriber licensed by a board (in Maryland or another state) may use the continuing education (CE) credits applied toward that board toward the Board of Pharmacy's CE requirements.

Sec. 10.34.18.06. Accredited Continuing Education Programs

The Board and the following providers are approved for any programs they offer which otherwise qualify for continuing education (CE) credit:

- o American Council on Pharmaceutical Education (ACPE).
- o Schools of pharmacy accredited by ACPE.
- o Food and Drug Administration (FDA).
- o Drug Enforcement Administration (DEA); and
- o Additional providers of programs approved by the Board.

Procedures for Approval of Additional Programs.

- o An additional provider shall request approval for an individual program by submitting a Board application at least 60 days before the date of offering of their individual program.
- o An approval request shall fulfill the program requirements set forth in Health Occupations Article, §12-309(g), Annotated Code of Maryland.
- o An approval request shall include a description of course work including:
  - ▪ Measurable learning objectives.
  - ▪ A course outline; and

- Self-assessment questions.
    - o The Board's decision to approve or disapprove a program is final.
- Record Keeping for Providers of Approved Programs.
- Providers of approved programs shall maintain program records for 3 years from the date of presentation of the program.
- Providers of approved programs of CE shall furnish a certificate of completion to participants who qualify. The provider shall include the:
    - o Name of the participant.
    - o Name of the provider.
    - o Title of the course.
    - o Number of CE hours.
    - o Date of completion; and
    - o A program identification number or provider number on the certificate.
- The Board may rescind approval of a CE program if it determines that the program no longer meets the requirements of Health Occupations Article, §12-309, Annotated Code of Maryland.

Sec. 10.34.18.07. Acceptance of Previously Unapproved Continuing Education Programs

- A pharmacist who completes a program of continuing education that is not previously approved by the Board may request in writing that the Board approve the program for credit.
- The pharmacist making a request for Board approval under §A of this regulation shall make the request at least 90 days before licensed expiration.

Sec. 10.34.18.08. Miscellaneous

- Credits may not be carried over from one licensing renewal period to another.

- Falsifying continuing education CE records is grounds for disciplinary action.

- The pharmacist shall use a Board approved form to supply the pharmacist's CE information to the Board.

- CE requirements imposed by the Board upon a pharmacist as part of an informal action, consent order, or final order, as defined in COMAR 10.34.01.02, shall be in addition to the requirements of this chapter.

- Pharmacists may receive 2 CE credits for attending a public Board meeting in its entirety.
  - The Board shall issue a certificate of proof of attendance at a public Board meeting.
  - A pharmacist may not earn more than 4 CE credits per renewal period for attendance of a public Board meeting.

Sec. 10.34.19.05. General Requirements

A licensed pharmacist who has appropriate practical and didactic training in compounding sterile preparations, clean room technology, laminar flow technology, quality assurance techniques, and clinical application of intravenous drug therapy shall control and supervise the section of the pharmacy that prepares compounded sterile preparations and is responsible for, at a minimum, the following:

- Preparation of compounded sterile preparations within the pharmacy or decentralized pharmacy.

- Storage of materials pertinent to the preparation of compounded sterile preparations, including drugs, chemicals, and biologicals, and the establishment of specifications for procurement of the materials.

- Labeling of containers of compounded sterile preparations compounded within the pharmacy.

- Recording of transactions of the pharmacy as may be applicable to State and federal laws and regulations, as may be necessary to maintain accurate control over, and accountability for, pharmaceutical materials; and

- Ensuring that licensed pharmacists meeting the requirements of §A of this regulation, or registered pharmacy technicians under direct supervision of a licensed pharmacist meeting the requirements of §A of this regulation, prepare, compound, and dispense compounded sterile preparations.

Sec. 10.34.19.06. Special Handling, Packaging, Labeling, and Beyond Use Dating

The pharmacy shall make available special handling and packaging materials to maintain container integrity and drug stability of the prepared prescription orders, including antineoplastic or other hazardous sterile preparations, during handling and administration to the patient including:

- A reasonable effort to provide tamper-evident packaging if appropriate to setting.
- Proper in-transit storage consistent with preparation labeling; and
- Delivery to the patient within a reasonable time.

- The dispensed container for any compounded sterile preparation shall include labeling according to Maryland law and regulations, in addition to the following information that is required by federal law:
  - The date of preparation unless otherwise readily retrievable from prescription records.
  - Time prepared, if applicable.
  - The pertinent requirements for proper storage.

- o The name of the prescriber, unless in an inpatient hospital setting.

- o The name of the patient.

- o Directions for use.

- o The name of the base solution for infusion preparations.

- o The name and concentration or amount of active drugs contained in the final sterile preparation.

- o The name or identifying initials of the pharmacist who checked or prepared the compounded sterile preparation unless otherwise readily retrievable from prescription records.

- o The name, address, and telephone number of the pharmacy unless in an inpatient hospital facility.

- o The beyond-use/expiration dating and time of the compounded sterile preparation, and if no time is stated, the time is presumed to be at 11:59 p.m. of the stated beyond use date.

- o Any ancillary and cautionary instructions as needed; and

- o A pertinent warning consistent with applicable federal and State law that cytotoxic preparations are biohazardous, when applicable.

- A pharmacy compounding sterile infusion preparations shall provide a 24-hour telephone number to allow its patients or other health care providers who may be administering its prescriptions to contact its pharmacists

Sec. 10.34.19.07. Record-Keeping Requirements

Patient Prescription Records.

The pharmacy shall maintain records of patient prescriptions.

- o Patient prescription records shall contain:

    - Available medical information consistent with prevailing pharmacy standards; and

    - The complete record of the formulations of the solutions that were compounded.

- The pharmacy shall keep completed patient prescription records in a retrievable manner for at least 5 years, either:

    - o At the inspection site; or

    - o So as to be immediately retrievable by computer or other electronic means.

Compounded Sterile Preparations Records.

- For a pharmacy preparing compounded sterile preparations, the following records shall be maintained for at least 5 years:

    - o The training and competency evaluation of employees in sterile preparation procedures.

    - o Refrigerator and freezer temperatures.

    - o Certification of the sterile compounding environment, including ISO 5 workstations and the clean and anterooms.

- o Other facility quality control logs specific to the pharmacy's policies and procedures, for example, cleaning logs for facilities and equipment.

- o Records documenting inspection for expired or recalled pharmaceutical preparations or raw ingredients.

- o Preparation records including compounding work sheets, and records of the registered pharmacy technicians' checking/sign-off process; and

- o Preparation records including compounding work sheets and records of the pharmacists' checking/sign-off process.

- In addition to the records requirement in §B(1) of this regulation, for batch compounded sterile preparations, a pharmacy compounding sterile batch preparations for future use shall have records indicating the:

  - o Drug and ingredient names.

  - o Lot numbers.

  - o Expiration dates.

  - o Drug/diluent amounts; and

  - o Date on which the compounded sterile batch preparations were prepared.

- A pharmacy shall maintain records of media fill verification results for 5 years.

Sec. 10.34.19.08. Batch Preparation

- A pharmacist may prepare batched sterile preparations for future use in limited quantities supported by prior valid prescriptions or physician orders before receiving a valid written prescription or medication order.

- Batch preparation of specific compounded sterile preparations is acceptable if the:

    o Pharmacist can document a history of valid prescriptions or physician orders that have been generated solely within an established professional prescriber-patient-pharmacist relationship; and

    o Pharmacy maintains the prescription on file for such preparations dispensed.

Sec. 10.34.19.09. Minimum Facility Requirements Latest version.

- Controlled Environment.

    o The pharmacy shall have a controlled environment that meets USP 797 Standards

    o A pharmacist shall ensure that the controlled environment is:

- Accessible only to designated personnel; and

- Used only for the preparation of compounded sterile preparations, or such other tasks that require a controlled environment.

    o The permit holder shall ensure that the controlled environment is:

    o Structurally isolated from other areas within the pharmacy by means of restricted entry or access; and

    o Air conditioned to maintain a temperature of the controlled environment according to USP 797 standards.

- Controlled Environment - Clean Room. The permit holder shall ensure that the clean room in the controlled environment:

    o Meets USP 797 Standards for design and USP 797 performance criteria quality standards for clean rooms.

    o Contains no sinks or floor drains.

- Contains work surfaces constructed of smooth, impervious materials, such as stainless steel or molded plastic, so that the work surfaces may be readily cleaned and sanitized.

- If cytotoxic agents are routinely used in compounding preparations, contains room or rooms equipped with special pressurization requirements consistent with USP 797 Standards and the National Institute for Occupational Safety and Health (NIOSH) standards.

- Has in place appropriate environmental engineering control devices capable of maintaining USP 797 air-quality standards during normal compounding activity; and

- Contains the following equipment:

  - A laminar airflow workstation or other suitable International Standards Organization (ISO) Class 5 compounding environment.

  - Waste containers that are approved by Occupational Safety and Health Administration (OSHA) for used needles and syringes, and for chemotherapy waste; and

  - Ancillary supplies required for proper compounding.

- Controlled Environment - Anteroom. The permit holder shall ensure that the anteroom in the controlled environment:

  - Meets USP 797 Standards for design and USP 797 performance criteria quality standards for anterooms: and

- Contains the following equipment:

  - A sink with hot and cold running water.

  - Waste containers for personal protective equipment.

- o An eyewash station or sink design suitable for flushing an eye injury; and

- o A hazardous waste spill kit, if applicable.

- The requirements specified in §§B(1) and C(1) of this regulation are not applicable if a compounding aseptic isolator is used to compound sterile preparations in accordance with the:

  - o Compounding aseptic isolator conditions set forth in USP 797 Standards: and

  - o Isolator vendor or manufacturer specifications.

Sec. 10.34.19.10. Minimum Requirements for Equipment

- The permit holder shall provide at least the following equipment that is maintained in working order:

  - o Adequate refrigerator and freezer space (if applicable).

  - o A sink and wash area in the anteroom.

  - o Appropriate waste containers for:

    - ▪ Used needles and syringes; and

    - ▪ Cytotoxic waste including disposable apparel used in its preparation, if applicable.

- Laminar air flow workstation or compounding aseptic isolator that meets USP 797 Standards, dedicated for products other than antineoplastics.

- If applicable to types of preparations compounded, biological safety cabinet, or compounding aseptic isolator that meets USP 797 Standards, dedicated for use with antineoplastics or other hazardous sterile preparations.

- Appropriate filters and filtration equipment; and

- A device for light/dark field examination.

- If used, the permit holder shall provide the following equipment that is maintained in working order, calibrated, or certified where appropriate:

  o Autoclave.

  o Automated compounding devices (for example, total parenteral nutrition compounding pumps)

  o Electronic balance.

  o Convection oven.

  o Thermometers or other temperature device; an

  o Incubator.

Sec. 10.34.19.11. Minimum Requirements for Supplies

A pharmacy engaging in compounding sterile preparations shall maintain adequate stock levels of the following supplies according to USP 797 Standards, including but not limited to:

- Personal protective equipment:

  o Sterile gloves.

  o Masks.

  o Non-shedding gowns.

  o Shoe covers.

  o Hair covers.

  o Beard covers; and

  o Other personal protective equipment.

- Disposable syringes and needles in necessary sizes.

Disinfectant cleaning agents as specified in USP 797 Standards, including 70 percent sterile isopropyl alcohol

- Disposable lint free towels.

- Hand washing materials, including antimicrobial skin cleanser.

- Adequate equipment and materials for antineoplastic or cytotoxic agent spills

- Supplies necessary for the aseptic preparation of compounded sterile preparations; and

- Closed system vial transfer devices (CSTD), as required for cytotoxic compounding, if applicable.

Sec. 10.34.19.12. Minimum Requirements for Policies and Procedures

The permit holder shall ensure that the pharmacist or the pharmacist's designee shall maintain a policy and procedure manual, reviewed annually, that sets forth in detail the permit holder's standard operating procedures with regard to compounding sterile preparations.

- The permit holder shall insure that the policy and procedure manual that sets forth the standard operating procedures with regard to compounding sterile preparations is implemented and adhered to.

- The policy and procedure manual shall include policies and procedures governing the following:
  - A risk-management program which includes documentation of outcomes including, but not limited to:
  - An incident reporting system.
  - An adverse drug reaction reporting system; and

- o   A preparation contamination reporting system.

- Security measures ensuring that the premises where sterile compounded preparations are stored and prepared are secured, to prevent access by unauthorized personnel.

- Equipment including, but not limited to:

    - o   Procedures for use.

    - o   Documentation of appropriate certifications; and

    - o   Documentation of appropriate calibration and preventive maintenance if applicable.

- Sanitation standards and procedures including monitoring for bacterial microorganisms to demonstrate effectiveness of cleaning activities.

- Reference materials as set forth in Regulation .16 of this chapter.

- Information concerning drug:

    - o   Preparation.

    - o   Storage and handling.

    - o   Dispensing.

    - o   Labeling.

    - o   Beyond-use/expiration dating.

    - o   Delivery.

    - o   Destruction.

    - o   Recalls; and

Returns.

- Patient record keeping as set forth in Regulation .07 of this chapter.

- Handling, dispensing, and documentation of investigational drugs.

- A quality assurance program.

- Verification of training and competency guidelines.

- Compounding process media fill verification procedures.

- Description of appropriate garb.

- Conduct guidelines for personnel in the controlled areas.

- Personnel responsibilities.

- Patient education, if appropriate.

- Protocol and procedures to maintain the integrity of the interior work area of the laminar air flow workstations.

- Written procedures as applicable for handling antineoplastic agents and other hazardous substances including:

  o Utilizing the proper equipment and supplies.

  o A statement that compounding shall be conducted within a properly certified biological safety cabinet or negative pressure compounding aseptic isolator.

  o Proper use of protective attire; and

  o Proper techniques to prevent both contamination of the preparation and chemical exposure of the individual preparing the prescription.

- Written procedures as applicable for the disposal of infectious materials or materials containing cytotoxic residues, or hazardous waste.

- Written documentation of policy and procedure changes based on data gathered from quality assurance evaluations; and

- Written documentation of policies and procedures assuring the sterility and stability of compounded sterile preparations.

Sec. 10.34.19.13. Attire

- When compounding sterile preparations, individuals shall comply with the following standards:
  - Sequencing of garbing that complies with USP 797 Standards.
  - Thorough handwashing before gowning.
  - Wearing clean room garb inside the designated area at all times, which consists of:
    - A non-shedding coverall or gown.
    - Head and facial hair covers.
    - A face mask; and
    - Shoe covers.
- Clean room garb, with the exception of sterile gloves, shall be donned and removed outside the designated clean room area.
- All jewelry shall be removed.
- Sterile gloves are required; and
- Make-up may not be worn in the clean room.
- The requirements of this regulation are not applicable if a compounding aseptic isolator is used to compound sterile preparations in accordance with USP 797 Standards and isolator vendor/manufacturer specifications.

Sec. 10.34.19.14. Training of Staff, Patient, and Caregiver

- The pharmacist shall make counseling available to the patient or primary caregiver, or both, concerning proper use of compounded sterile preparations and related supplies furnished by the pharmacy.

- The permit holder shall ensure that pharmacy personnel engaging in compounding sterile preparations are trained and demonstrate competence in the safe handling and compounding of compounded sterile preparations and parenteral solutions, including cytotoxic agents if applicable.

- The permit holder shall maintain records of training and demonstrated competence for individual employees for 5 years.

- The permit holder shall ensure the continuing competence of pharmacy personnel engaged in compounding sterile preparations.

- A pharmacy that compounds sterile preparations shall comply with the following training requirements:

  o The pharmacy shall establish and follow a written program of training and performance evaluation designed to ensure that individuals working in the designated area have the knowledge and skills necessary to perform the assigned tasks properly and include at least the following:

    ▪ Aseptic technique with media fill verification at a frequency defined by risk level as described in USP 797 Standards:

      • 12 months for low and medium risk; and

      • 6 months for high risk.

    ▪ Pharmaceutical calculations and terminology.

  o Compounding sterile preparation documentation process.

  o Quality assurance procedures.

  o Aseptic preparation procedures.

  o Proper cleansing, gowning, and gloving techniques.

- o General conduct in the controlled area.

- o Cleaning, sanitizing, and maintaining equipment used in the controlled area.

  - ▪ Sterilization techniques for high-risk preparations; and

- o Container, equipment, and closure system selection.

- Individuals assigned to the controlled area shall successfully complete practical skills training in aseptic technique and aseptic area practices.

- Evaluations shall include:

  - o Written testing.

  - o Observation for adherence to aseptic technique and aseptic area policies and procedures; and

  - o Media fill verification as set forth in §E(1)(a) of this regulation.

Sec. 10.34.19.15. Quality Assurance

The permit holder shall ensure that the compounded sterile preparation retains its potency and sterility throughout the assigned "beyond use" dating period through a written quality assurance program that includes:

- A reasonable effort by the pharmacist to assure that compounded sterile preparations shall be kept under appropriate controlled conditions before dispensing, during transport, and at the location of use by providing adequate labeling and verbal or written instructions regarding proper storage and administration, as set forth by the product manufacturer and established standards and literature, with each compounded sterile preparation dispensed.

- The phases of compounded sterile preparation, distribution, storage, administration, and directions for use for each type of preparation dispensed.

- Environmental sampling for microbial organisms in laminar air flow workstations and clean rooms is performed according to methods and schedules specified by USP 797 Standards and if microbial contamination is suspected, for example, in the event of positive media fill verification results.

- Laminar air flow workstations, biological safety cabinets, and compounding aseptic isolators certified by a trained and qualified operator.

- Clean room and anteroom certification by a trained and qualified operator according to USP 797 Standards.

- The proper disposal in accordance with accepted professional standards and applicable State and federal laws of unused drugs and materials used in the preparation of compounded sterile preparations, including antineoplastic agents and hazardous materials.

- A formal written review process to report and evaluate compliance with this chapter; and

- A process that complies with applicable USP 797 Standards for performing sterility checks or pyrogen testing, or both, for applicable compounded sterile preparations.

Sec. 10.34.19.16. Reference Library

Minimum reference materials in a pharmacy shall include:

- U.S. Pharmaceutical, General Chapter 797, Pharmaceutical Compounding-Sterile Preparations and other applicable reference materials in order to perform sterile compounding.

- Reference materials containing drug stability and compatibility data; and

- Reference materials concerning drug interactions and incompatibility.

Sec. 10.34.19.17. Minimum Requirements for Inspections

- The Board shall inspect pharmacies located in Maryland at least annually.

- The pharmacy shall provide as part of the inspection process:

    o Quality assurance testing reports.

    o Documentation of reporting adverse events as required in Regulation .18 of this chapter.

    o Microbial testing of a sampling of the sterile compounded preparations of the pharmacy if applicable according to USP 797 Standards; and

    o Any other information requested to ensure compliance with USP 797 Standards.

- Within 90 days before the date of application, inspections of nonresident pharmacies may be conducted by:

    o A designee of the Board.

    o The U.S. Food and Drug Administration; or

    o Another appropriate state entity which indicates compliance with USP 797 Standards.

- The Board or designee shall inspect nonresident pharmacies upon initial application and upon renewal.

- The Board may inspect a pharmacy at any time to:

    o Verify compliance with permit requirements; or

    o Investigate a complaint.

Sec. 10.34.19.18. Reporting Requirements Pharmacies

A pharmacy shall:

- Document and perform routine testing as required by USP 797 Standards for the appropriate risk levels of sterile compounded preparations: and

- Report to the Board within 5 calendar days:

  o Adverse events that have been discovered including corrective actions taken or proposed.

  o Deficiencies related to the sterile compounding process.

  o Disciplinary actions in other states or by other state agencies.

  o Changes in accreditation status.

  o Disciplinary actions taken against a pharmacist who is an owner, operator, or employee of the pharmacy; and

  o Disciplinary actions taken against any other known permit, or any other authorization, held by the pharmacy permit holder.

Sec. 10.34.19.19. Office Use

Unless otherwise authorized, a person that prepares and distributes sterile compounded medications for office use into, out of, or within the State shall hold:

- A manufacturer's permit or other permit designated by the U.S. Food and Drug Administration to ensure the safety of sterile compounded medications for office use; and

- If applicable, a wholesale distributor's permit, issued by the Board under Health Occupations

Article, Title 12, Subtitle 6C, Annotated Code of Maryland. Chapter 10.34.20. Format of Prescription Transmission

Sec. 10.34.20.02. Requirements for Prescription

- A valid prescription shall be:
  - Valid in the professional judgment of the pharmacist responsible for filling the prescription; and
  - Conveyed:
    - In a manner that contains the handwritten, pen-to-paper signature of the prescriber.
    - In a manner that is transmitted to the pharmacy electronically, provided that the prescription is:
      - Transmitted via electronic intermediaries that are certified by the Maryland Health Care Commission.
      - Received by the permit holder's computer, facsimile machine, or other electronic device; and
      - Maintained by the permit holder in accordance with Regulation .03 of this chapter; or
    - In an oral manner where:
      - Only a pharmacist may take an original oral prescription by a voice messaging system or by phone with the pharmacist reading back the prescription to the prescriber or the prescriber's agent; and
      - The pharmacist promptly reduces the oral prescription to writing.

- The requirement of §A(2)(b)(i) of this regulation does not apply to prescriptions transmitted electronically within:

    o A closed system of a group model health maintenance organization as defined in Health-General Article, §19-713.6, Annotated Code of Maryland; or

    o Any other closed system that does not utilize an intermediary for transmission of prescriptions.

Sec. 10.34.20.03. Prescription Records

The pharmacy permit holder shall maintain prescription records in a form that:

- Is readily and accurately retrievable.

- Is maintained for at least 5 years from the date of dispensing; and

- Protects the confidentiality and security of the prescription information.

Sec. 10.34.20.04. Controlled Dangerous Substances

Transmission and dispensing of controlled dangerous substances shall be in accordance with applicable State and federal statutes and regulations.

Chapter 10.34.21. Standard of Practice for Unlicensed Personnel

Sec. 10.34.21.03. Duties of the Permit Holder

The permit holder shall:

- Determine which operational support tasks the pharmacist may assign unlicensed personnel to perform in the prescription area.

- Ensure that unlicensed personnel:

- o Receive appropriate training for the tasks that the pharmacist assigns unlicensed personnel to perform in the prescription area.

- Receive training that will enable unlicensed personnel to understand how the provisions of Health-General Article, Title 4, Subtitle 3, Annotated Code of Maryland, apply to:

  - o Prescription records, and

  - o The requirements for confidentiality of patient specific information; and

- When performing tasks in the prescription area, maintain proper:

  - o Sanitation.

  - o Hygiene.

  - o Biohazard precautions; and

  - o Infection control; and

- Ensure that unlicensed personnel are clearly identified to the consumer.

Sec. 10.34.21.04. Duties of the Pharmacist

- The pharmacist shall provide supervision to unlicensed personnel.

- The pharmacist may not delegate any pharmacy acts to unlicensed personnel.

Sec. 10.34.21.05. Duties of Unlicensed Personnel

- Unlicensed personnel under the supervision of a pharmacist may perform operational support which the unlicensed personnel have been trained to adequately perform in the prescription area.

- Unlicensed personnel who perform duties in the prescription area shall maintain the confidentiality of patient specific data in accordance with Health-General Article, Title 4, Subtitle 3, Annotated Code of Maryland.

Sec. 10.34.21.06. Grounds for Discipline

- A pharmacist licensee may be subject to discipline if the pharmacist licensee violates any provision of Regulation .04 of this chapter.

- A permit holder may be subject to disciplinary action if:

  - The permit holder fails to take reasonable safeguards to ensure compliance with the regulations of the Board; or

- The permit holder otherwise violates any of the provisions of Regulation .03 of this chapter.

Sec. 10.34.22.03. Minimum Application Requirements for Applicants Holding Product

- The Board shall require the following minimum information from a wholesale distributor as part of an application for a permit and as part of a renewal of a permit:

  - The type of business form under which the applicant operates, such as partnership, corporation, or sole proprietorship.

- The full name or names of the owner and the operator of the wholesale distributor applying for or renewing a permit, including:

  - For an individual, the:

    - Full name of the individual.

    - Telephone number of the individual.

    - Business address of the individual; and

    - Date of birth of the individual.

  -

- For a partnership, the:

  - Full name of each partner.

  - Telephone number of the partnership.

  - Address of each partner.

  - Date of birth of each partner.

  - Business address of the partnership; and

  - Federal employer identification number of the partnership.

- For a publicly traded corporation, the:

  - Full name and title of each corporate officer and director.

  - Telephone number of the publicly traded corporation.

  - Business address of the corporation.

  - Federal employer identification number of the corporation.

  - Name of parent company or companies if applicable.

  - Corporate names.

  - Name of the state of incorporation; and

  - Name and address of the resident agent of the corporation.

- For a nonpublicly traded corporation, the:

  - Full name and title of each corporate officer and director.

  - The telephone number of the nonpublicly traded corporation.

  - Business address of the corporation.

  - Federal employer identification number of the corporation.

  - Name of parent company or companies if applicable.

  - Corporate names.

- Full name and business address of shareholders of more than 10 percent of the corporation, including over-the-counter stock, unless the stock is traded on a major stock exchange.

- Name of the state of incorporation; and

- Name and address of the resident agent of the corporation.

o For a sole proprietorship, the:

- Full name of the sole proprietor.

- The telephone number of the sole proprietor.

- Full name of the business entity.

- Business address; and

- Date of birth of the sole proprietor.

o For a limited liability company, the:

- Full name and business address of the limited liability company.

- Telephone number of the limited liability company.

- Full name of each member.

- Full name of each manager.

- Federal employer identification number of the limited liability company.

- Name of the state in which the limited liability company was organized; and

- Name and address of the resident agent of the company.

- Addresses, telephone numbers, and the names of contact persons for the facility used by the applicant for the storage, handling, and distribution of prescription drugs.

- All trade or business names used by the permit holder which may not be identical to the name used by another unrelated applicant in the State.

- A list of federal and state licenses, registrations, or permits, including the license, registration, or permit numbers issued to the wholesale distributor by federal authority or another state that authorizes the wholesale distributor to purchase, possess, and distribute prescription drugs or devices.

- A list of disciplinary actions by federal or state agencies against the wholesale distributor as well as any such actions against principals, owners, directors, or officers.

- For the designated representative and the immediate supervisor of the designated representative at the applicant's place of business the following information:

  o Names.

  o Places of residence for the past 7 years.

  o Dates and places of birth.

  o The name and address of each business where the individual was employed during the past 7 years, and the individual's job title or office held at each business.

  o A statement of whether, during the past 7 years, the individual has been the subject of any proceeding for the revocation of any professional or business license or any criminal violation and, if so, the nature and disposition of the proceeding.

  o A statement of whether, during the past 7 years, the individual has been enjoined, either temporarily or permanently, by a court of competent jurisdiction from violating any federal or state law regulating the possession, control, or distribution of prescription drugs, together with details concerning the event.

- A description of any involvement, including any investments other than the ownership of stock in a publicly traded company or mutual fund, by the individual during the past 7 years, with any business that manufactures, administers, prescribes, distributes, or stores prescription drugs, and any lawsuits in which the business was named as a party.
- A description of any misdemeanor or felony offense of which the individual, as an adult, was found guilty, regardless of whether adjudication of the guilt was withheld or whether the individual pled guilty or nolo contendere.
  - If the individual indicates that a criminal conviction is under appeal and submits a copy of the notice of appeal, within 15 days after the disposition of the appeal, a copy of the final written order of disposition: and
  - A photograph of the individual taken in the previous 180 days.

- A full description of the facility and warehouse including:

  - Square footage.

  - Security and alarm system descriptions.

  - Terms of lease or ownership.

  - Address; and

  - Description of temperature and humidity controls.

  - Written evidence that the wholesale distributor has obtained general and product liability insurance.

  - A description of the wholesale distributor's import and export activities; and

  - Other relevant information that the Board may require.

Sec. 10.34.22.03-1. Minimum Application Requirements for Virtual Manufacturers

The information and qualification requirements for obtaining a permit under Regulation .03 of this chapter, beyond that required by federal law, do not apply to a virtual manufacturer that meets the following requirements:

- Provides a list of drug or device products it distributes.

- Provides a list of the NDA or ANDA numbers associated with each drug it distributes.

- Provides a list of the UDI numbers, as available, associated with each device it distributes.

- Provides the name and facility address of the contract manufacturer for each drug or device product it distributes.

- Provides verification of current FDA registration for each contract manufacturing facility listed.

- If the contract manufacturer distributes into this State, provides the wholesale distributor permit number for the contract manufacturer.

- If the contract manufacturer does not distribute into this State, provides name and Maryland's wholesale distributor permit number for the entity that physically distributes the product into this State.

- Provides a statement affirming that the virtual manufacturer does not contract the manufacture or distribution for drugs or devices other than those for which it owns the NDA, ANDA, or UDI numbers.

- Provides an attestation by the owner of the virtual manufacturer that it does not hold product.

- Provides a copy of existing licensure from the state in which it is located, if applicable; and

- Has valid federal licensure or registration, as verified by the Board.

Sec. 10.34.22.04. Personnel Latest version.

- The permit holder shall affirm in the initial application and subsequent renewal applications that personnel employed in wholesale distribution have appropriate education and experience to assume responsibilities related to compliance with State licensing requirements.

- Registered Agent.

  o Each licensed wholesale distributor located outside of this State that wholesale distributes prescription drugs or devices in this State shall designate a registered agent in this State for service of process.

  o If any wholesale distributor is not licensed in this State, service on the Director of the State Department of Assessments and Taxation only shall be sufficient service.

- Requirements and Responsibilities of the Designated Representative.

- The designated representative shall be aware of, and knowledgeable about, all policies and procedures pertaining to the operations of the wholesale distributor, including applicable State and federal laws.

- The designated representative shall have documented training sufficient to ensure that operations of the wholesale distributor are in compliance with applicable State and federal laws and are provided by qualified in-house specialists, outside counsel, or consulting specialists with capabilities to help ensure compliance with all applicable State and federal laws and regulations.

- The designated representative shall maintain current working knowledge of the requirements for wholesale distributor and assure ongoing training for personnel to ensure compliance.

- The designated representative shall be responsible for all record keeping requirements and make all records available for inspection.

Sec. 10.34.22.05. Violations and Penalties

- After a hearing held under Health Occupations Article, §12-601, Annotated Code of Maryland, the Board may deny, suspend, revoke, or place on probation a permit holder, reprimand a permit holder, or impose a fine if the permit holder:
    - Is convicted of, or pleads guilty or nolo contendere to, violations of federal, State, or local drug or device laws or regulations.
    - Is convicted of, or pleads guilty or nolo contendere to, a felony or to a crime involving moral turpitude, whether or not any appeal or other proceeding is pending to have the conviction or plea set aside.
    - Commits any of the following acts:
        - Obtains or attempts to obtain a permit by:
            - Providing false information to the Board; or
            - Other fraudulent or deceptive means.
        - Fails to:
            - Establish or maintain inventories, records, or written policies and procedures as required by Regulation .07 of this chapter.
            - Register with the Maryland Division of Drug Control, and with the U.S. Drug Enforcement Agency, as required by Regulation .07D of this chapter; or

- Permit the Board, the Maryland Division of Drug Control, the U.S. Drug Enforcement Agency, or other authorized federal, State, or local law enforcement officials showing proper identification, to enter, inspect, copy records, or audit as required by Regulation .07D of this chapter.

- Willfully makes or maintains false inventories or records.

- Violates a provision of, or regulation promulgated under, Health Occupations Article, Title 12, Annotated Code of Maryland.

- Manufactures, repackages, sells, delivers, or holds or offers for sale any prescription drug or device that is adulterated, misbranded, counterfeit, suspected of being counterfeit, or has otherwise been rendered unfit for distribution or wholesale distribution.

- Adulterates, misbrands, or counterfeits prescription drugs or devices.

- Receives prescription drugs or devices that are adulterated, misbranded, stolen, obtained by fraud or deceit, counterfeit, or suspected of being counterfeit, or delivers or proffers delivery of such prescription drug or device for pay or otherwise.

- Alters, mutilates, destroys, obliterates, or removes the whole or any part of the product labeling of a prescription drug or device, or commits any other act with respect to a prescription drug or device that results in the prescription drug or device being misbranded.

- Forges, counterfeits, simulates, or falsely represents prescription drugs or devices without the authority of the manufacturer, or uses any mark, stamp, tag, label, or other identification device without the authorization of the manufacturer.

- Purchases or receives a prescription drug or device from a person who is not licensed to wholesale distribute prescription drugs or devices to that purchaser or recipient.

- Sells or transfers a prescription drug or device to a person who is not legally authorized to receive a prescription drug or device.

- Provides the Board, its representatives, or federal or State officials with false or fraudulent records or makes false or fraudulent statements regarding any matter within the provisions of these regulations.

- Wholesale distributes prescription drugs or devices that were:

    o Purchased by a public or private hospital, or other health care entity.

    o Donated or supplied at a reduced price to a charitable organization.

    o Stolen or obtained by fraud or deceit; or

    o Donated to a drop-off site or repository under the Prescription Drug Repository Program set forth in Health-General Article, Title 15, Subtitle 6, Annotated Code of Maryland.

- Fails to obtain a license or operates without a valid license when a license is required.

- Obtains, or attempts to obtain, a prescription drug or device by fraud, deceit, misrepresentation, or engages in misrepresentation or fraud in the distribution or wholesale distribution of a prescription drug or device.

- Distributes a prescription drug or device to a consumer or patient.

- Fails to obtain, authenticate, or pass on a pedigree when required under these regulations

- Receives a prescription drug pursuant to a wholesale distribution without first receiving a pedigree, when required, that was attested to as accurate and complete by the wholesale distributor.

- Distributes or wholesale distributes a prescription drug or device that was previously dispensed by a pharmacy or distributed by a practitioner.

- Fails to report prohibited acts as listed in these regulations.

- Fails to exercise due diligence as provided in Regulation .08 of this chapter.

- Otherwise conducts the wholesale distribution of prescription drugs or devices in a manner not in accordance with the law.

- Accepts payment or credit for the sale of prescription drugs in violation of Health Occupations Article, §12-6C-09(d), Annotated Code of Maryland; or

- If the requirements of Health Occupations Article, §12-6C-09(a), Annotated Code of Maryland, are applicable and are not met, the purchasing or otherwise receiving a prescription drug from a pharmacy; or

- Is disciplined by a licensing or disciplinary authority of any state or country or disciplined by a court of any state or country, for an act that would constitute a ground for Board action against a wholesale distributor permit holder under §A or B of this regulation.

- Acts prohibited under this regulation do not include a prescription drug manufacturer, or agent of a prescription drug manufacturer, obtaining or attempting to obtain a prescription drug for the sole purpose of testing the prescription drug for authenticity.

Prescription Drugs.

○ If the conditions under which a prescription drug has been returned cast doubt on the prescription drug's safety, identity, strength, quality, or purity, then the wholesale distributor shall destroy or return the prescription drug to the supplier, unless examination, testing, or other investigation proves that the prescription drug meets appropriate standards of safety, identity, strength, quality, and purity.

- o In determining whether the conditions under which a prescription drug has been returned cast doubt on the prescription drug's safety, identity, strength, quality, or purity, the wholesale distributor shall consider, at a minimum, the:

  - Conditions under which the prescription drug has been held, stored, or shipped before or during its return; and

  - Condition of the prescription drug and its container, carton, or labeling, as a result of storage or shipping.

- Prescription Devices.

  - o If the conditions under which a prescription device has been returned cast doubt on the prescription device's safety, identity, or quality, then the wholesale distributor shall destroy or return the prescription device to the supplier, unless examination, testing, or other investigation proves that the prescription device meets appropriate standards of safety, identity, strength, and quality.

  - o In determining whether the conditions under which a prescription device has been returned cast doubt on the prescription device's safety, identity, or quality, the wholesale distributor shall consider, among other things, the:

    - Conditions under which the prescription device has been held, stored, or shipped before or during its return; and

    - Condition of the prescription device and its container, carton, or labeling, as a result of storage or shipping.

- A wholesale distributor shall follow the record-keeping requirements in Regulation .07 of this chapter for outdated, damaged, deteriorated, misbranded, or adulterated prescription drugs or devices.

Sec. 10.34.22.08. Due Diligence

Wholesale distributors having transactions with persons not licensed by the Board or not certified by a third party recognized by the Board shall have in place policies and procedures to perform due diligence on transactions that take place that include:

- Verification of alternate licensure.

- Verification of identity; and

- Verification of recent inspections by a state or third-party entity recognized by the Board.

Sec. 10.34.22.09. Reinstatement

- The wholesale distributor permit shall expire on the last day of its term.

- The Board may not reinstate the wholesale distributor permit unless the applicant pays a reinstatement fee set by the Board.

Sec. 10.34.22.11. Relocation

At least 30 days before relocation, a permit holder shall submit an application to the Board.

- If relocation is due to a catastrophic event or State of Emergency, the relocation applicant shall:

- o Notify the Board within 48 hours; and

- o Submit an application to the Board within 30 days.

- A relocation applicant:

  - o If the applicant holds products, shall comply with Regulation .07 of this chapter.

  - o Shall submit a surety bond or other equivalent means of security acceptable to the State specific to the permit holder's relocation, in accordance with Regulation .03 if this chapter; and

  - o Shall indicate on the application changes in product or personnel from the original application to the Board

- A new or different designated representative or immediate supervisor of a designated representative functioning at the relocated facility shall be required to undergo a criminal history records check as set forth in Regulation .03 of this chapter.

- As part of the application process, a relocation applicant located in this State shall submit to and pass an opening inspection conducted by the Board, which shall include:

  - o Documentation of the permit holder's notification to suppliers of prescription drugs and devices of the permit holder's relocation; and

  - o Documentation from the permit holder evidencing the appropriate transfer, return, or disposal of any prescription drugs or devices not transferred to the facility's relocation.

- A relocation applicant located in another state shall provide to the Board:

  - o Evidence of approval of the permit holder's relocation from the accreditation organization that accredited the permit holder's original location; or

  - o If the relocation applicant is not required to be accredited by an accreditation organization in accordance with Maryland law, inspection reports from the state in which the relocation applicant is located pertaining to the permit holder's relocation.

Sec. 10.34.28.04. Usage Requirements for Centralized Automated Medication Systems

- An automated medication system may only be used if:
  - Records concerning transactions or operations are maintained in accordance with Regulation .11 of this chapter.
  - A responsible pharmacist has been designated by the permit holder to supervise and manage the operations of the centralized automated medication system; an
  - The permit holder ensures that:
    - Patients have prompt access to pharmacy services necessary for the provision of good pharmaceutical care as defined in Health Occupations Article, §12-101, Annotated Code of Maryland.
    - The centralized automated medication system maintains the integrity of the information in the system and protects patient confidentiality; and
    - The centralized automated medication system is subject to a quality assurance program in accordance with Regulation .10 of this chapter.
- A permit holder shall indicate on the initial, renewal, and reinstatement applications:
  - Whether the permit holder operates a centralized automated medication system; and
  - Any other information regarding the system that the Board considers necessary to determine compliance with this chapter.

Sec. 10.34.28.05. Usage Requirements for Decentralized Automated Medication Systems

- A decentralized automated medication system may only be used if:

  o Records concerning transactions or operations are maintained in accordance with Regulation .11 of this chapter.

  o A responsible pharmacist has been designated by the permit holder to supervise and manage the operations of the automated medication system.

  o Except for starter doses, a licensed pharmacist reviews each order for medication:

    ▪ After the order has been entered into the system; and

    ▪ Before the system permits access to the medication.

  o The permit holder ensures that:

    ▪ Patients have prompt access to pharmacy services necessary for the provision of good pharmaceutical care as defined in Health Occupations Article, §12-101, Annotated Code of Maryland.

    ▪ The decentralized automated medication system maintains the integrity of the information in the system and protects patient confidentiality; and

    ▪ The decentralized automated medication system is subject to a quality assurance program in accordance with Regulation .10 of this chapter; and

  o It is designed to distribute medications in a licensed health care facility, a related institution as defined in Health-General Article, §19-301, Annotated Code of Maryland, or a medical facility owned and operated by a group model health maintenance organization as defined in Health-General Article, §19-713.6, Annotated Code of Maryland.

- A starter dose, or a dose in response to an emergency, may be distributed without prior review by a pharmacist of the order if:
  - The pharmacist reviews the order within 24 hours of removal from the decentralized automated medication system; or
  - The prescriber reviews the patient medical history and authorizes the administration of the dose to the patient.

- Decentralized automated medication systems shall operate in a manner which:
  - Limits simultaneous access to multiple:
    - Drug strengths.
    - Dosage forms; or
    - Drug entities

- Prevents access to medications not ordered for the patient; and

- Safeguards against the misidentification of medications, dosages, and dosage forms by those accessing the decentralized automated medication system.

- The requirements listed in §C (1) and (2) of this regulation do not apply to automated supply towers which contain:
  - Noncontrolled medications that are:
    - Refrigerated.
    - Bulk; or
    - Intravenous fluids; o
  - Prescription devices

- A permit holder shall indicate on the initial, renewal, and reinstatement applications:

  o Whether the permit holder operates a decentralized automated medication system; and

  o Any other information regarding the system that the Board considers necessary to determine compliance with this chapter.

Sec. 10.34.28.07. Stocking of Automated Medication Systems

Selection of Medication for Stocking.

- A licensed pharmacist shall verify the accuracy of medications selected for stocking and replenishment of the automated medication system before the medications are stocked in the system.

Stocking of Automated Medication System.

- A registered pharmacy technician may stock an automated medication system provided that:

  o The pharmacy technician's selection of medications is verified by a pharmacist; and

  o The system uses positive drug identification such as bar code technology.

Section 10.34.29.02 - Content of Protocol

A protocol shall: Be: Written; an

- Condition or disease-state specific; and contain the following

  o The condition that the protocol is designed to manage.

  o A list of medications that may be used under the auspices of the protocol

- o Monitoring parameters including laboratory tests for the:
    - Condition; and
    - Medication employed.
- A list of circumstances requiring contact with the authorized prescriber or authorized prescribers who are a party to the prescriber-pharmacist agreement.
    - o A statement prohibiting substitution of a chemically dissimilar drug product by the pharmacist for the product prescribed by the authorized prescriber unless permitted in the therapy management contract
    - o A list of circumstances under which the pharmacist may alter doses, modify the treatment regimen, or switch the agent under the terms of the therapy management contract.
    - o Information to be documented
    - o A listing of provisions within the protocol that may be customized within a therapy management contract; and
        - An action plan for situations when the pharmacist encounters a situation that is not addressed in the protocol.
- A protocol may authorize:
    - o The modification, continuation, and discontinuation of drug therapy.
- The ordering of laboratory tests
- Other patient care management measures related to monitoring or improving the outcomes of drug or device therapy; an
- For protocols by a licensed physician and licensed pharmacist, the initiation of drug therapy under written, disease-state specific protocols.

o A protocol may not authorize acts that exceed the scope of practice of the parties to the prescriber-pharmacist agreement

o Technical modifications to the protocol shall be registered with the Board of Pharmacy within 30 days of the technical modification.

Section 10.34.30.01 - Application for Name Change

The name of an individual or entity required to possess a pharmacy or wholesale distribution permit may be changed on a permit if:

- The permit holder submits a notice of name change to the Board within 30 days after the name change, on a form that the Board requires

- The permit holder submits to the Board documentation verifying the name change; an

- There is no other change in the individual or entity required to possess a pharmacy or wholesale distribution permit including no change in controlling ownership interest, type of business entity, or location.

Section 10.34.30.01 - Application for Name Change

The name of an individual or entity required to possess a pharmacy or wholesale distribution permit may be changed on a permit if:

- The permit holder submits a notice of name change to the Board within 30 days after the name change, on a form that the Board requires.

- The permit holder submits to the Board documentation verifying the name change; an

- There is no other change in the individual or entity required to possess a pharmacy or wholesale distribution permit including no change in controlling ownership interest, type of business entity, or location.

Section 10.34.30.04 - Applications for Pharmacy or Wholesale Distributor Establishment Change of Location

- Permits issued to operate a pharmacy or engage in wholesale distribution, whether located in the State or outside the State, are:
  - Not transferable; and
  - Specific to the establishment location that has undergone an opening inspection by the Board.

- A pharmacy or wholesale distributor that intends to change its establishment location shall:
  - Submit an application to the Board on a form required by the Board.
  - If located in the State, comply with opening and closing inspection requirements in order to:
    - Commence operations at the new establishment location; and
    - Cease operations at the existing establishment location; and

- If located outside the State, submit an inspection report for the new location conducted by the authorized entity in the state in which the establishment is located, or provide documentation of supplemental accreditation, if applicable.

Section 10.34.30.05 - Change of Information Provided in Applications

Notwithstanding any other reporting requirements, a permit holder shall provide written notification to the Board at least 30 days prior to any change in information in its application provided to the Board, to include:

- Change in hours of operation.

- Change in the physical structure of the establishment, to include any:
  - Deviation from the floor plan submitted by the permit holder as part of the application; or
  - Other change that may affect the security or storage conditions of prescription drugs or devices.

Section 10.34.30.06 - Incomplete Applications

- The Board may hold an incomplete initial or reinstatement application for a license, registration, or permit for up to one year from the date of receipt.

- After 1 year from the date of receipt, the Board shall close a pending application that is incomplete

- If an application has been closed under §B of this regulation, the applicant shall submit a new application fee and otherwise comply with all applicable license, registration, or permit requirements.

- If an applicant presents extenuating circumstances to the Board, the Board may, in its sole discretion, extend the 1-year application completion period.

Section 10.34.31.01 - Settings

- If a setting otherwise complies with State and federal laws, a pharmacist may request Board approval to dispense or distribute at a setting that does not possess a pharmacy permit if:

  o The dispensing or distribution occurs while the pharmacist is providing drug therapy management services in:

    - The office of a licensed physician.

    - A clinic; or

    - A medical facility; or

  o The setting is:

    - Operated or funded by a public health authority of the State.

    - A medical facility or clinic that is operated on a nonprofit basis and is not otherwise required to possess a pharmacy permit, o

    - A health center that operates on a campus of an institution of higher education.

- If the drug therapy management services referred to in §A(1)(a) of this regulation include the dispensing or distribution of controlled dangerous substances, the request may be approved by the Board if the physician possesses a dispensing permit issued by the Board of Physicians

- If a pharmacist seeks to obtain Board approval to dispense or distribute at a setting that is not set forth in §A of this regulation, the pharmacist shall apply to the Board for a waiver permit under COMAR 10.34.17.

Section 10.34.31.02 - Pharmacist Approval

- Before a pharmacist may dispense or distribute at a setting that does not hold a pharmacy permit under Regulation .01A (1) of this chapter, the pharmacist shall submit to the Board a request for approval signed by the pharmacist, which includes:
    - The name and license number of the pharmacist.
    - The scope of services to be provided by the pharmacist at the nonpharmacy setting.
    - The name and address of the nonpharmacy setting where the pharmacist intends to dispense or distribute; and
    - A statement indicating the pharmacist's criminal history if any
- If the pharmacist intends to provide drug therapy management services in a licensed physician's office under Regulation .01A(1)(a) of this chapter, in addition to the requirements of §A of this regulation, the pharmacist shall provide:
    - The name and license number of the licensed physician; an
    - Proof of an approved physician-pharmacist agreement with the licensed physician.

Section 10.34.38.03 - Prohibited Pharmacy Acts

A registered pharmacy intern may not:

- Delegate a pharmacy act.
- Perform a final verification of a prescription drug or device before dispensing
- Perform any act that has not been authorized by the supervising pharmacist
- Represent themselves as a pharmacist
- Dispense prescription medications when the pharmacist is not in the pharmacy

- Be present in the pharmacy when the pharmacist is not physically available onsite

- Act within the parameters of a therapy management contract as provided under Health Occupations Article, Subtitle 6A, Annotated Code of Maryland

- Independently compound prescriptions; or

I Accept the return of prescription drugs or devices directly from a patient

Section 10.34.38.04 - General Requirements

Each registered pharmacy intern shall:

- o Display the pharmacy intern's registration in the office or place of business in which the pharmacy intern is practicing pharmacy under the direct supervision of a licensed pharmacist; or

- o Have the registration on the pharmacy intern's person available for viewing

- When practicing pharmacy under the direct supervision of a licensed pharmacist, the registered pharmacy intern shall wear identification that conspicuously identifies the registered pharmacy intern as a registered pharmacy intern.

- When performing tasks in the prescription area, a pharmacy intern shall maintain proper:
  - o Sanitation.
  - o Hygiene
  - o Biohazard precautions; and
  - o Infection control.

- A pharmacy intern, who has obtained a registration as an actively enrolled student, shall immediately notify the Board if the pharmacy intern's enrollment as a student has been revoked, suspended, terminated, or otherwise discontinued.

Section 10.34.38.06 - Registration Requirements

- An applicant shall be an individual who:

    o Is currently enrolled and has completed 1 year of professional pharmacy education in a Doctor of Pharmacy program:

        - Accredited by the Accreditation Council for Pharmacy Education; or

        - Having precandidate or candidate status by the Accreditation Council for Pharmacy Education.

- Has graduated from a Doctor of Pharmacy program accredited by the Accreditation Council for Pharmacy Education; or

- Is a graduate of a foreign school of pharmacy who:

    o Has established educational equivalency as approved by the Board; and

    o Has passed an examination of oral English approved by the Board

- An applicant identified in §A of this regulation shall:

    o Submit to the Board a signed completed application on a form provided by the Board.

    o Pay a fee as set forth in COMAR 10.34.09.

    o Submit a request for a State Criminal History Records check; an

    o Be of good moral character

- The Board may not approve an application until the State Criminal History Records Check is completed

- The Board of Pharmacy shall provide the pharmacy intern with a registration card and pocket identification card upon initial registration and renewal.

Section 10.34.38.07 - Renewal Requirements

- The pharmacy intern's registration shall expire on the last day of the birth month following 1 year after initial registration.

- Except as provided in §C of this regulation, the Board shall send to each registrant, at least 1 month before a registration expires, a renewal notices by first-class mail to the last known address of the registrant.

- If requested by a registrant, the Board shall send to the registrant, at least two times within the month before a registration expires, a renewal notice by electronic means to the last known electronic address of the registrant

- If a renewal notice sent by electronic means under §C of this regulation is returned to the Board as undeliverable, the Board shall send to the registrant a renewal notices by first-class mail to the last known address of the registrant.

- A renewal notice sent under this regulation shall state:

  o The date on which the current registration expires.

  o The date by which the renewal application must be received by the Board for the renewal to be issued and mailed before the registration expires; and

  o The amount of the renewal fee

- A registered pharmacy intern who qualifies for registration under Regulation .06A (1) of this chapter may renew the registration one time if the registered pharmacy intern is:

  o Otherwise entitled to be registered as a pharmacy intern.

  o Submits to the Board a renewal application on the form that the Board requires; and

  o Pays to the Board a renewal fee set by the Board

- A registered pharmacy intern who qualifies for registration under Regulation .06A(2) and (3) of this chapter may not renew the registration

- The registration of a pharmacy intern registered under this chapter is void when the registered pharmacy intern becomes a licensed pharmacist

- The Board shall renew the registration of each pharmacy intern who meets the requirements of this chapter.

Section 10.34.40.03 - Requirements to Prescribe Contraceptives

- Board Responsibilities. The Board shall develop and adopt the following items, in consultation with stakeholders to be determined by the Board:
    - A self-screening risk assessment questionnaire that a patient shall complete before a pharmacist may prescribe contraceptives for a patient.
    - A standard procedure contraceptive algorithm which the pharmacist shall use to perform a patient assessment for purposes of determining:
        - Whether to prescribe contraceptives; and
        - Which contraceptive options to prescribe.
- A notification form to be submitted by a pharmacist before prescribing contraceptives; and
- Other forms and procedures for:
    - The prescription of contraceptives; and
    - Referral to a primary care or reproductive health care practitioner for treatment.
- Notification.
    - A pharmacist who has undergone training for prescribing contraceptives as part of the pharmacist's formal educational program:

- Is exempt from completing a Board-approved training program; and

- At least 15 days before prescribing contraceptives, shall submit to the Board a notification form, which includes an attestation of the pharmacist's formal education program.

  o A pharmacist may not prescribe contraceptives until the pharmacist receives a written confirmation from the Board accepting the pharmacist's notification form

- Pharmacist Responsibilities.

For each new patient requesting contraceptive services, and at a minimum of every 12 months for each returning patient, a participating pharmacist shall:

- Obtain the completed Board-approved self-screening risk assessment questionnaire from the patient; and

- Utilize and follow the Board-approved standard procedure contraceptive algorithm to

  - Perform the patient assessment.

  - Determine whether to prescribe contraceptives; and

  - Determine which contraceptive options to prescribe.

- Upon completion of all requirements established by the Board and after review of all relevant information, a pharmacist may prescribe contraceptives, if deemed clinically appropriate

- If contraceptives are prescribed, the pharmacist shall:

- Refer the patient:

- For additional care to their primary care practitioner or reproductive health care practitioner; or

- If the patient does not have a primary care practitioner or a reproductive health care practitioner, to a family planning provider or a licensed clinician who provides reproductive health care services.

- Provide the patient with a visit summary; and

Document the encounter and maintain records pursuant to Regulation .05 of this chapter

- Upon completion of all requirements established by the Board and after review of all relevant information, if the pharmacist does not prescribe contraceptives, the pharmacist will provide a visit summary to the patient which provides the basis for the decision not to prescribe contraceptives.

- A pharmacist may not prescribe contraceptives before January 1, 2019.

Section 10.34.40.04 - Training Program Requirements

At a minimum, a Board-approved training program shall contain the following elements:

- An overview of contraceptive medications and self-administered contraceptive devices

- An overview of the self-screening risk assessment questionnaire

- An overview of the standard procedure contraceptive algorithm; an

- An overview of the U.S. Medical Eligibility Criteria for Contraceptive Use and other Center for Disease Control guidance on contraception.

Section 10.34.40.05 - Record Keeping

For a minimum of 5 years, a pharmacy whose pharmacists prescribe contraceptives shall maintain documentation, in electronic or other form, which includes:

- The type of contraceptive prescribed, and dosage, if applicable, or the basis for not prescribing a contraceptive.

- The name, address, and date of birth of the patient.

- The name of the pharmacist who prescribed the contraceptive or determined a contraceptive would not be prescribed

- The date the contraceptive was prescribed or that the patient was advised that a contraceptive would not be prescribed

- A copy of the patient's visit summary.

- A copy of the patient's self screening risk assessment questionnaire; and

- The name and address of the:

  - Patient's primary care practitioner or reproductive health care practitioner, if provided by the patient, o

  - Family planning provider or licensed clinician who provides reproductive health care services referred by the pharmacist, if the patient does not have a primary care practitioner or reproductive health care practitioner.

Section 10.34.40.06 - Continuing Education Requirement

- A pharmacist who prescribes contraceptives in Maryland shall earn 1 hour of Board-approved continuing pharmaceutical education related to contraception before the pharmacist's license renewal date.

PART-TWO

MARYLAND PHARMACY LAW QUESTIONS

1. Which DEA form is used when a pharmacy uses a reverse distributor to dispose of outdated controlled substances?

    b. DEA form 41

    c. DEA from 106

    d. DEA from 222

    e. DEA form 224

2. Which schedule has no medicinal use?

    a. Schedule I

    b. Schedule II

    c. Schedule III

    d. Schedule IV

3. Medicare _____ provides prescription coverage.

    a. Part A

    b. Part B

    c. Part C

    d. Part D

4. What is the schedule for 1.8 grams of codeine in a 100 ml solution?

    a. Schedule II

    b. Schedule III

    c. Schedule IV

    d. Schedule V

5. Per Federal laws, how long does the pharmacy keep records of schedule II drugs?

    a. 2 years

    b. 3 years

    c. 5 years

    d. 7 years

6. On October 30, 2019, a patient comes to pick up a refill on Ambien 10 mg prescription dated March 1, 2018. What would you do as a pharmacist based on Federal law?

    a. Fill

    b. Do not fill

    c. Fill 72-hours supply only

    d. Fill a onetime fill only and tell the patient to see the prescriber

7. Long-term detoxification treatment should not be longer than:

    a. 30 days

    b. 60 days

    c. 120 days

    d. 180 days

8. Per Federal laws, in order to buy pseudoephedrine related OTC Schedule V drugs, the purchaser should be at least _____ old.

   a. 16 years

   b. 18 years

   c. 21 years

   d. 23 years

9. A prescription of Amlodipine 10mg, # 30, written by Dr. John from out of state with valid and full prescriptive authority presented to you at pharmacy in the state you are currently working as a pharmacist. What course of action would you take?

   a. Fill the prescription.

   b. Don't fill. The quantity is in excess legally allowed.

   c. Don't fill. Prescription from out of state is NOT valid.

   d. Don't fill. It is illegal to fill control substance from out of state.

10. According to federal laws, what is the minimum time between an initial and third purchase of schedule V OTC drug?

    a. 24 hours

    b. 48 hours

    c. 72 hours

    d. 120 hours

11. What are the total days of supply of Simvastatin 20 mg prescription that may be dispensed with authorized refills, as long as it doesn't exceed the total quantity authorized by the prescriber?

    a. 30 days

    b. 60 days

    c. 90 days

    d. 120 days

12. Per Federal law what is the quantity limit of schedule II drugs to be dispensed at a time?

    a. 30 days

    b. 60 days

    c. 90 days

    d. 120 days

13. What is the schedule for 500 mg of opium in a 100 ml solution?

    a. Schedule II

    b. Schedule III

    c. Schedule IV

    d. Schedule V

14. A pharmacist receives a prescription for 40 Percocet tablets, but the pharmacy has only 15 tablets in stock. The patient accepts the 15 tablets. How much time does the pharmacist have to provide the remaining 25 tablets per Federal law?

   a. 24 hours

   b. 72 hours

   c. 96 hours

   d. 6 months

15. A member of the Air Force who is authorized to administer, prescribe or dispense a controlled substance during official duties is required to register with DEA on:

   a. Every 6 months

   b. Annually

   c. Biennially

   d. Exempt from registration

16. DEA form 222 kept for inspection for:

   a. 2 years

   b. 3 years

   c. 4 years

   d. 5 years

17. Responsibilities for the dispensing of controlled substances is upon:

    I.   The prescriber.

    II.   The pharmacist.

    III.   The pharmacy

    a. I only

    b. III only

    c. I and II

    d. II and III

18. Per Federal laws, what is the maximum amount of opium a pharmacist can sell as an OTC drug?

    a. 100 ml

    b. 120 ml

    c. 240 ml

    d. 360 ml

19. How many times a refill prescription can be transferred between pharmacies sharing a real-time on-line database for Diazepam 5 mg prescription with FOUR refills on it?

    a. 3 refills

    b. 4 refills

    c. 5 refills

    d. 10 refills

20. Which of the following medications needs an estimated count for purpose of inventory?

    I.   An opened container of morphine 5 mg that holds around 80 tablets

    II. An opened container of Norco 5/325 tab that holds around 75 tablets

    III. An opened container of Vimpat that holds around 30 tablets

    a. I only

    b. I and II only

    c. III only

    d. I, II, and III only

21. The prescription for an inpatient of a skilled nursing facility must be rendered and at least partially filled

    within _____ following the date of issue.

    a. 30 days

    b. 60 days

    c. 90 days

    d. 120 days

22. What is the schedule for 50 mg of morphine in a 100 ml solution?

    a. Schedule II

    b. Schedule III

    c. Schedule IV

    d. Schedule V

23. Per Federal laws, Marijuana is classified as:

    a. Schedule I

    b. Schedule II

    c. Schedule III

    d. Schedule IV

24. What is DEA form 106 used for?

    a. Disposal of controlled substances.

    b. Ordering Schedule II medications.

    c. Theft or loss of controlled substances.

    d. Reporting inventory levels of controlled substances.

25. How many refills are allowed for Xanax?

    a. 3 refills in 6 months

    b. 4 refills in 6 months

    c. 5 refills in 6 months

    d. 6 refills in 5 months

26. If the drug is labeled August 2020, what date does the drug expire?

    a. 08/01/2020

    b. 08/31/2020

    c. 07/01/2020

    d. 07/31/2020

27. A pharmacist receives a prescription for methylphenidate 5 mg written by a dentist for a patient. What course of action would you take as a pharmacist?

   a. Fill the prescription

   b. Don't fill. Dentist only prescribes methylphenidate 10 mg.

   c. Don't fill. Dentist only prescribes Adderall.

   d. Don't fill. The prescription is out of scope practice.

28. Carisoprodol is classified as

   a. Schedule II

   b. Schedule III

   c. Schedule IV

   d. Schedule V

29. A physician's agent cannot call in for a prescription for:

   a. Lorazepam

   b. Pregabalin

   c. Dronabinol

   d. Hydromorphone

30. What is DEA Form 41 used for?

   a. To report the theft of controlled substances.

   b. To document the destruction of controlled substances.

   c. To report the inventory levels of controlled substances.

   d. To order schedule II drugs.

31. What is the maximum day supply of the medication the pharmacy can dispense for an emergency situation like natural disaster fill?

    a. 10 days

    b. 14 days

    c. 30 days

    d. 60 days

32. Per Federal law, what is the limit for schedule II day of supply?

    a. 30 days

    b. 90 days

    c. 120 days

    d. No limit

33. Which form is used when ordering morphine ER 60?

    a. DEA 41

    b. DEA 106

    c. DEA 222

    d. DEA 225

34. Medicaid/Medicare records of patient's are required to be stored for at least:

    a. 5 years

    b. 7 years

    c. 10 years.

    d. 12 years.

35. Which of the following drugs is exempt from the PPPA locking cap requirements?

    a. Varenicline

    b. Topiramate

    c. Pregabalin

    d. Nitroglycerin

36. A prescriber may authorize a maximum of how many refills on a prescription for Percodan tablets?

    a. 0

    b. 1

    c. 2

    d. 5

    e. 10

37. What is the schedule for 200 mg of codeine in a 100 ml solution (including non-narcotic ingredients)?

    a. Schedule II

    b. Schedule III

    c. Schedule IV

    d. Schedule V

38. An exact count is allowed for schedule IV product in a container that holds greater or equal to

_____ capsules or tablets.

 a. 500

 b. 1000

 c. 1500

 d. 2000

39. What is the maximum day of supply of lorazepam that may be prescribed by a physician?

 a. 30 days

 b. 60 days

 c. 90 days

 d. None of the above.

40. On Saturday night, Dr. John telephoned in an emergency prescription of Percocet for a patient. Three

tablets were dispensed. How long does Dr. John have to present a written prescription for this order?

 a. 48 hours

 b. 72 hours

 c. 7 days

 d. Sch. II orders cannot be telephoned.

41. The expiration date on a bottle of Naproxen is 6/2020. When will this drug expire?

    a. June 30, 2020.

    b. June 1, 2020

    c. June 15, 2020

    d. July 30, 2020

42. A prescription of Lipitor 10 mg is valid for:

    a. 3 months

    b. 6 months

    c. 9 months

    d. 12 months

43. A patient brings a prescription for Diazepam 10 mg to a pharmacy. Upon reviewing a profile, the prescription has already been refilled 5 times. The pharmacy technician will do which of the following?

    a. Refill the prescription as it was written prn times.

    b. Cannot refill. Notify the pharmacist.

    c. Refuse to fill since the prescription needs the DEA Form 222.

    d. Refuse to fill since the drug is NOT in a stock.

44. The term "donut hole" refers to which of the following situations?

  a. Prescription drug costs to the beneficiary before reaching the catastrophic coverage

  b. The period of time during which a person may enroll in Plan D

  c. The period of time during which a beneficiary may change health insurance companies

  d. A dollar range in which the beneficiary must pay for all prescription drugs

45. Under which of the following circumstances, can the pharmacist dispense a faxed prescription of Percocet 10/325 mg?

  I.   The patient of a Long-Term Care Facility (LTCF)

  II. The patient is in hospice care

  III. The patient is diagnosed with a terminal illness

  IV. The patient is undergoing home infusion/IV pain therapy

  a. I and II only

  b. II and III only

  c. III and IV only

  d. I, II, III, and IV

46. A practitioner may dispense directly to ultimate user a controlled substance classified in Schedule II in an amount not to exceed:

    a. 48-hours supply

    b. 72-hours supply

    c. 120-hours supply

    d. 180-hours supply

47. All prescription records for non-controlled substances shall be maintained on the licensed premises for a period of _____ from the date of dispensing.

    a. 1 year

    b. 2 years

    c. 3 years

    d. 4 years

48. A prescription for Xanax is valid for:

    a. 4 months

    b. 5 months

    c. 6 months

    d. 12 months

49. Which USP chapter addresses compounding non-sterile products?

    a.   USP <790>

    b.   USP <795>

    c.   USP<797>

    d.   USP<800>

50. A prescriber may authorize a maximum of how many refills on a prescription for Percodan tablets?

    a.   0

    b.   1

    c.   2

    d.   5

51. What is the maximum number of refills for Soma prescriptions in a six-month period?

    a.   2

    b.   3

    c.   4

    d.   5

52. Which of the following is an example of 3 file storage system?

    a. Schedule I, Schedule II- III, Schedule V

    b. Schedule II, Schedule III-V, Non-scheduled

    c. Schedule I, Schedule II- V, Non-scheduled

    d. Schedule II, Schedule III, Schedule IV, Schedule V

53. In non-emergency situations, a pharmacist may dispense an oral prescription received from a duly

    authorized agent of a practitioner for all of the following drugs EXCEPT:

    a. Lorazepam

    b. Lyrica

    c. Vimpat

    d. Cocaine

54. If a prescription is written for a 90-day supply, then what is the expiration term for this prescription?

    a. Original plus 2 refills

    b. Original plus 3 refills

    c. Original plus 4 refills

    d. Original plus 11 refills

55. Which of the following is TRUE about Schedule II drug class?

    I.   Refills are not allowed.

    II.   Multiple 30-day script written on the same day are allowed, if the total amount does not exceed 90 days.

    III.   Changing patient name not allowed by the pharmacist.

    IV.   Partial fills are allowed, if completed within 72 hours.

    a.   I and II only

    b.   II and III only

    c.   III and IV only

    d.   I, II, III, and IV

56. Dr. Adam called in for emergency fill of Percocet 10/325. What do you do?

    a.   Fill up to 90 days' supply

    b.   Don't fill

    c.   Oral prescription of C-II is illegal.

    d.   Physician can call in schedule II drug in case of emergency

57. When a pharmacist partially fills controlled substance II, the remaining portion of a schedule II prescription may be filled within:

    a.   24-hours of the first partial filling.

    b.   36-hours of the first partial filling.

    c.   48-hours of the first partial filling.

    d.   72-hours of the first partial filling.

58. Which of the following medications requires an exact count as an inventory?

    a. Soma

    b. Vimpat

    c. Halcion

    d. Percocet

59. According to federal law, DEA forms need to be maintained for _____ years.

    a. 1

    b. 2

    c. 5

    d. 7

60. A prescription of allopurinol 100 mg, # 180 prescribed for "office use" by Dr. Bilal: What course of action would you take?

    a. Fill the entire prescription

    b. Only fill 30 tablets

    c. Fill after verifying the prescription

    d. Don't fill. Prescription for office use is not acceptable.

61. If a pharmacy partially fills a schedule II prescription, upon each partial fill the pharmacist must document:
    I.   Date of fill.

    II. The quantity dispensed.

    III. The remaining quantity.

    IV. The pharmacist's sign.

a. I and II only

b. II and III only

c. III and IV only

d. I, II, III, and IV

62. The supplier of oxycodone 10 mg has time to send shipment to purchaser within:

    a. 10 days

    b. 15 days

    c. 30 days

    d. 60 days

63. A prescription for Xanax 2mg may be refilled how many times?

    a. 1

    b. 2

    c. 3

    d. 5

64. Which form is used to report lost or stolen drugs?

    a. DEA 41

    b. DEA 222

    c. DEA 224

    d. DEA 106

65. Which DEA form is used to report the theft or loss of controlled substances?

   a. DEA Form 69

   b. DEA Form 224b

   c. DEA Form 41

   d. DEA Form 106

66. Which of the following is TRUE about schedule II prescription?

   I.   It can be refilled.

   II.   It can be transferred.

   III.   It can be faxed.

   IV.   It can be emailed.

   a. II only

   b. III only

   c. IV only

   d. None of the above.

67. An authorized prescriber must mail a copy of an emergency oral prescription for a schedule II drug

   within_____ after an oral authorization.

   a. 72 hours

   b. 7 days

   c. 14 days

   d. 30 days

68. The prescriber is mandated to return the hardcopy prescription within _____ days after giving over the phone schedule II emergency supply per Federal law.

    a. 24 hours

    b. 72 hours

    c. 7 days

    d. 10 days

69. Mr. David comes in with a prescription for Diazepam dated today. How many refills allowed per controlled substance act law?

    a. 1 time only

    b. 3 times in 5 months

    c. 6 times in 5 months

    d. 5 times in 6 months

70. Recalled drugs must be removed from inventory within _____ hours of the recall notification.

    a. 12 hours

    b. 24 hours

    c. 36 hours

    d. 72 hours

71. The prescription for a terminally ill patient must be tendered and at least partially filled

within_____ following the date of issue.

    a.   30 days

    b.   60 days

    c.   90 days

    d.   120 days

72. Emergency contraception treatment may be prescribed up to_____ of unprotected intercourse.

    a.   12 hours

    b.   48 hours

    c.   120 hours

    d.   150 hours

73. The partial filling of Morphine 15 mg for terminally ill patient must be done within _____

from the initial filling.

    a.   72 hours

    b.   144 hours

    c.   30 days

    d.   60 days

74. Which of the following covers inpatient hospitals stays?

    a.   Medicare Part C

    b.   Medicare Part B

    c.   Medicare Part A

    d.   Medicare Part D

75. Waxman hatch has extended the patent period of:

    a.   14 years

    b.   17 years

    c.   5 years

    d.   8 years

PART TWO

ANSWER TO MARYLAND PHARMACY LAW

1. Answer: C

   DEA form 222 is used when disposing of controlled substances through a reverse distributor.

2. Answer: A

   Schedule I drug has no medical use.

3. Answer: D

   Medicare Part D provides prescription drug coverage.

4. Answer: B

   1.8 grams of codeine in a 100 ml solution is a schedule III drug.

5. Answer: A

   Per Federal laws, the pharmacy keeps records of schedule II drugs for 2 years

6. Answer: B

   Prescriptions for schedule IV-controlled substance drugs may be refilled for 6 months from the date of the prescription if refills have been authorized by the prescriber.

7. Answer: D

   Long-term detoxification treatment should not be longer than 6 months or 180 days.

8. Answer: B

   Per Federal laws, the purchaser should be at least 18 years old.

9. Answer: A

   Prescription order for non-control legend drug from out-of-state prescriber is valid as long as the prescriber has full prescribing authority.

10. Answer: B

   According to federal laws, it is 48 hours.

11. Answer: C

   A pharmacy may dispense accelerated refills of up to a 90-day supply of medication pursuant to a valid prescription that may be dispensed with authorized refills, as long as it doesn't exceed the total quantity authorized by the prescriber.

12. Answer: C

   There is 90-day supply limit to all schedule II drugs per federal laws.

13. Answer: B

   500 mg of opium in a 100 ml solution is a schedule III drug.

14. Answer: B

   The Controlled Substances Act allows for the partial filling of a Schedule II medication prescription, with the remaining medication to be provided to the patient within 72 hours or the quantity becomes void.

15. Answer: D

   The requirement of registration is waived for any official or agency of the U.S. Army, Navy, Marine Corps, Air Force, Coast Guard, or Public Health Service who or which is authorized to import or export-controlled substances in the course of his or her official duties.

16. Answer: A

   DEA form 222 kept for inspection for 2 years.

17. Answer: C

   Responsibility for the dispensing of controlled substance is upon the prescriber and the pharmacist.

18. Answer: C

   240 ml of opium can be sold by pharmacist as an OTC drug.

19. Answer: B

A maximum of 4 refill prescription can be transferred between pharmacies sharing a real-time on-line database for a schedule IV drug prescription like diazepam 5 mg with FOUR refills on it.

20. Answer: C

The exact count is required for schedule I and II drugs in a commercial container which has been opened. The estimated count is required for schedule III to V drugs in a commercial container which has been opened.

21. Answer: B

The prescription for an inpatient of a skilled nursing facility must be rendered and at least partially filled within 60 days following the date of issue.

22. Answer: B

50 mg of morphine in a 100 ml solution is a schedule III drug.

23. Answer: A

Marijuana- Schedule I

24. Answer: C

Written notification must be provided to the DEA Field Division Office of the theft or significant loss of any controlled substance within one business day of discovery of the loss. DEA form 106 must be completed and submitted to the Field Division Office.

25. Answer: C

Xanax is classified as controlled substances (schedule IV).

26. Answer: B

The drug expires the last day of the month.

27. Answer: D

Prescribing ADHD medication is not in the ordinary course of professional practice of a dentist.

28. Answer: C

Carisoprodol- Schedule IV.

29. Answer: D

A physician's agent cannot call for schedule II drugs. In this case, hydromorphone.

30. Answer: B

The purpose of DEA Form 41 is to document the surrender of controlled substances that have been forwarded to the DEA for disposal.

31. Answer: C

The maximum day supply of the medication the pharmacy can dispense for an emergency situation like natural disaster fill is 30 days' supply.

32. Answer: D

Per Federal law, there is no limit for schedule II day of supply.

33. Answer: C

Morphine ER is schedule II drug. Therefore, DEA form 222 is used to order schedule II.

34. Answer is C

Records related to Medicaid/Medicare patients are required to be stored for at least. 10 years.

35. Answer: D

Examples include sublingual dosage forms of nitroglycerin, sublingual and chewable forms of isosorbide dinitrate in dosage strengths of 10 milligrams or less, anhydrous cholestyramine in powder form and others.

36. Answer: A

Schedule II drugs has no refills.

37. Answer: D

200 mg/100 ml of codeine solution is a schedule V drug.

38. Answer: B

> An exact count is allowed for schedule III- V products in a container that holds greater or equal to 1000 capsules or tablets.

39. Answer: D

> There is no limit on the quantity of schedule III-V controlled substances that can be prescribed by a physician.

40. Answer: C

> Federal require 7 days for the Dr. to present the written prescription to the dispensing pharmacy for oral prescription of controlled class-II.

41. Answer: A

> Drug expiration date is the last day of the month unless specifically stated for specific date.

42. Answer: D

> A prescription of Lipitor 10 mg is valid for 12 months or 1 year.

43. Answer: B

> A prescription for Schedule III and IV controlled drugs cannot be refilled more than 5 times within a period of six months from the date the prescription was issued. A patient must bring a new prescription since all the allowable refills were executed.

44. Answer: D

> A "donut hole" is a dollar range in which the beneficiary must pay for all prescription drugs

45. Answer: D

> The patient of a Long-Term Care Facility (LTCF), hospice care, patient diagnosed with a terminal illness and the patient undergoing home infusion/IV pain therapy are exception to schedule II faxed prescription.

46. Answer: B

> A practitioner may dispense directly to un ultimate user a controlled substance classified in Schedule II in an amount not to exceed 72-hours supply.

47. Answer: A

All prescription records for non-controlled substances shall be maintained on the licensed premises for a period of one year from the date of dispensing.

48. Answer: C

A prescription for schedule III to IV is valid for 6 months.

49. Answer: B

Non-sterile USP <795>

Sterile USP <797>

50. Answer: A

Schedule II drugs has no refills.

51. Answer: D

Soma has 5 refills, schedule IV.

52. Answer: B

3 file storage system means: Schedule II, Schedule III-V, Non-scheduled.

53. Answer: D

Schedule II drugs don't be dispensed via oral prescription in non-emergency situations.

54. Answer: B

90 days = 1 months plus 3 refills

55. Answer: D

All the above lists are correct about schedule II drug class.

56. Answer: D

Over the phone prescription of schedule II drugs can be filled in case of emergency.

57. Answer: D

When a pharmacist partially fills controlled substance II, the remaining portion of a schedule II prescription may be filled within 72-hours of the first partial filling.

58. Answer: D

Schedule II drug Percocet requires an exact count for inventory.

59. Answer: B

According to federal law, DEA forms need to be maintained for 2 years.

60. Answer: D

The prescription should not be filled because a prescription is the incorrect method to order drugs "for office use."

61. Answer: D

The pharmacist must document upon each partial fill:

- Date of fill.

- The quantity dispensed.

- The remaining quantity.

- The pharmacist's sign.

62. Answer: D

The supplier of oxycodone 10 mg has time to send shipment to purchaser within 60 days.

63. Answer: D

Schedule 4 drug and can be refilled 5 times.

64. Answer: D

Stolen medications reported via DEA form 106.

65. Answer: D

The DEA-106 is for reporting any theft or loss of controlled substances.

66. Answer: D

It cannot be refilled, transferred or faxed it can be faxed only on few exceptions.

67. Answer is B

Such prescription must be mailed within 7 days of such authorization

68. Answer: C

The prescriber is mandated to return the hardcopy prescription within SEVEN days after giving over the phone schedule II emergency supply.

69. Answer: D

Schedule III to V medications cannot be filled more than 5 times within 6 months.

70. Answer: B

Recalled drugs must be removed from inventory within 24 hours of the recall notification.

71. Answer: B

The prescription for a terminally ill patient must be tendered and at least partially filled within 60 days following the date of issue.

72. Answer: C

Emergency contraception treatment may be prescribed up to 120 hours of unprotected intercourse.

73. Answer: D

The partial filling of Morphine 15 mg for terminally ill patient must be done within 60 days from the initial filling.

74. Answer: C

Medicare Part A covers inpatient hospital stays, including a semiprivate room, food, and tests. The maximum length of stay that will be covered is usually 90 days.

75. Answer: C

Waxman hatch has extended the patent period of 5 years.

REFERENCES

1. UMB School of Pharmacy: pharmacy law review course and materials

2. NABP Pre-MPJE Practice Exam

3. Maryland Board of Pharmacy home page

4. Pharmacy Laws and Regulations for the State of Maryland book order form

5. Maryland Laws Pertaining to Pharmacy (not an exclusive list)

6. Health General (HG) Title 21 Subtitle 2. Maryland Food, Drugs, and Cosmetics Act

7. Health General (HG) Title 21 Subtitle 2A. Prescription Drug Monitoring Plan

8. Health Occupations (HO) Title 12. Pharmacists and Pharmacies

9. COMAR 10.34 - Board of Pharmacy Regulations

10. DEA's Diversion Control Division Website www.DEAdiversion.usdoj.gov

11. DEA Homepage www.dea.gov

12. U.S. Government Publishing Office

13. https://www.govinfo.gov Provides access to the CFR, Parts 1300 to End, primary source for the

    Pharmacist's Manual, and the Federal Register which contains proposed and finalized amendments to

    the CFR.

14. Office of National Drug Control Policy (ONDCP) www.whitehouse.gov/ondcp

15. Food and Drug Administration www.FDA.gov

16. SAMHSA www.samhsa.gov

17. CSAT https://www.samhsa.gov/about-us/who-we-are/offices-centers/csat

18. Federation of State Medical Boards www.FSMB.org

19. National Association of Boards of Pharmacy https://nabp.pharmacy

20. National Association of State Controlled Substances Authorities www.nascsa.org

Made in the USA
Middletown, DE
17 December 2024

67442964R00077